PRESENT-FUTURE
LEADER

How To Thrive In
Today's Economy

RANDALL WOLKEN

MACNY, The Manufacturers Association
5788 Widewaters Parkway
Syracuse, NY 13214
www.macny.org

ISBN – 9781717808165
Imprint – MACNY Books

DEDICATION

To the hardworking men and women of the manufacturing community. Your ingenuity and dedication to creating incredible products are the bedrock upon which we can – and do – build up our local communities.

TABLE OF CONTENTS

FOREWORD

Leadership is said to be a skill that can be learned from formal training, acquired through experience, and absorbed by observing others. The world of business and academia are filled with how-to books, can't miss seminars, scholarly treatise, and consulting gurus all willing to share their secrets, in order to make us better leaders. While all of this is important, its focus tends to be on what I call 'Leadership from the Head.' It often misses the 'Leadership from the Heart' aspect of being an effective leader.

I have known and worked beside Randy Wolken for 15 years, and he has developed a balanced understanding between 'Leadership from the Head' and 'Leadership from the Heart.' One focus of *Present-Future Leader* is that balance. Throughout this book, Randy addresses the 'Head' aspect such as in chapters 8 (*Is it Getting Done?*) and 9 *(Move Quickly and Keep Moving!)*, and also the 'Heart' as illustrated in chapters 13 (*Passion is Key!*) and 14 (*Love and Kindness as Competitive Advantages*).

As Randy defines Present-Future Leadership and differentiates it from our current day model of Past-Present Leadership, he makes a compelling case for speed of innovation and the amount of change that today's leaders are facing, and that the pace of change and innovation will only accelerate in the future. He notes that it is important that we honor the past. "Great leaders honor the past and the people who made it possible, while charting a path to a successful future." His challenge to us is what are we to do about the speed and pace needed to evolve from the old model to become the Present-Future Leader? By sharing stories and experiences he has heard and observed, he offers a path to successfully navigate this challenge.

In introducing the concept of a '4th *Industrial Revolution,*' or 4th wave of technological advances, Randy makes the case that as leadership shifts away from the Baby Boomers, Gen-Xers and Millennials are better equipped to handle the speed of change but still need the skills to be an effective leader. Fortunately for us Boomers, there is hope since excellence knows no age!

He also points out that in order to be successful in business and even in life itself, we need to embrace change and the pace of it, and be cognizant of the impact it will have on those around us. Since change is always with us, Randy uses the mechanism of our habits and how to change them throughout the rest of the book. We first facilitate change within ourselves, and then move outward to those we care about, then to those we influence, and finally to those we lead. By changing one habit or doing one kind act, one day at a time, we will place ourselves on the road to being a Present-Future Leader.

One last observation from 40 years of service in manufacturing: The quest to be an effective leader is a continuous journey that never ends. Allow this book to help you along the path.

Jim Beckman
Former MACNY Board Chair
Former President of Crucible

WHY I WROTE THIS BOOK

This book has been a dream of mine for a very long time. I truly love books – especially books about successful leaders, leadership, and professional growth. In these pages, I am able to share my understanding of how to lead in this turbulent and fast-paced economic climate. It is hard to be truly successful as a leader of an organization today. It has never been more difficult. And yet, I have witnessed some of the finest leadership examples within thriving companies anywhere on the planet. It's impressive. I have attempted to crystallize this for you, the reader.

I am absolutely convinced that everyone can be a leader and that they can help companies thrive today. I have seen what it takes. It is not rocket science. However, it is not easy either. Once a leader knows how to proceed and does so quickly and consistently, they can and will be wildly successful. I call it Present-Future Leadership. How do I know it works? I have seen it over and over again.

I want you, the reader, to know how to lead like a Present-Future Leader. What is that? Read on and you will find out.

But, before you do – a word of caution. Present-Future Leaders will need to change the way they lead in some meaningful ways. You cannot just do things the way you always have. Every leader today will need to change to thrive in today's economy. Do not get discouraged by this. The legendary leaders have all had to change to continue to be successful – every one of them!

Be legendary, we need you to do so. And, enjoy the journey – it can be quite a ride!

WHO HELPED
ME WRITE THIS BOOK

So many people made this book possible. I will attempt to capture the many individuals I am indebted to for their inspiration and assistance. I will certainly not be able to name them all. It would take me another book. But, I do want them – and you – to know just how grateful I am for their assistance and ongoing friendship. Relationships are the hallmark of satisfying and effective leaders. Leadership is more about influence than control. Our relationships define us as leaders. In this way, I am incredibly blessed.

First, my incredible wife Denise made this book possible. Her devotion to me and our family is simply amazing. For over three decades, she has been my best friend. I love her dearly. I also want to thank my amazing daughters – Annemarie, Christina, and Rebecca. I marvel at what caring and capable women they have become. Bravo! Finally, I want to thank my parents, Ron and Joan Wolken. They are responsible for the life I now live. They believed in me from the start. They, to this day, are my real-life heroes. Thanks!

I want to thank the MACNY Board of Directors and collective leaders and team members of the membership of MACNY – The Manufacturers Association. I have been privileged and blessed to serve the over 300 member companies of MACNY who collectively have over 100,000 employees. What an honor. I have learned so much from you. You are the inspiration for this book!

To write and prepare a book takes a team. First, I thank Marisa Norcross. She has been my editor for my weekly messages and monthly newsletter articles for the last few years. She performed the same incredible feat for this book. She makes me sound good – without eliminating my unique voice. She is truly amazing.

Also, I want to thank my wonderful staff and teammates at MACNY – Cindy Nave, Karyn Burns, David Freund, Mary Rowland, Patty Clark, Cindy Oehmigen, Marisa Norcross, Martha Ponge, Julianne Pease, Hilary Hext, Meghan McBennett, Arlene Hiltbrand, Andrea Riccelli, Joe Vargo, Kathy Birmingham, Jason Bjork, and Yaël Miller. You are such an inspiration to me and our members. Thanks!

Brian Bosché has been my book coach. He guided me in my development of this book and its contents – and how to do so quickly and effectively. Without Brian, I would not have even begun to write this book. His knowledge and encouragement made this book not only a possibility – but a reality. Hilary Hext has been instrumental in helping me complete the book on-time and to roll it out to the broader community. A special thanks to my daughter, Annemarie, who designed the cover art for this book. I would also like to thank Jim Beckman, the former President of Crucible. He wrote a wonderful foreword. He has been my guide, mentor, and friend for the better part of 15 years.

Special thanks go to Nate Andrews, Bill Allyn, LTC Bill Belich, Adolphe Nyakasane, Lou and Mark Steigerwald, and countless MACNY member company leaders who taught me how Present-Future Leaders act to create the most sustainable companies anywhere.

Finally, thank you – the reader – for spending the time to read this book. I wrote this book with you in mind. It is because of you I am inspired to share my insights. I hope you learn from it, apply its lessons, and enjoy it.

- 1 -

TODAY'S ECONOMY AND WORLD

I have a special view of the changing worldwide economy. For the past 16 years I have been the President and CEO of the largest manufacturers association in New York State. Hundreds of the most successful companies in the state and world are the member companies I serve daily. I have seen firsthand how successful leaders and companies have adjusted to the new economy. They share with me their strategies to thrive as individuals, leaders, and organizations. My goal is to share these insights with you, the reader.

So, what is happening in today's economy and world? For so many Baby Boomers (like me), it seems so confusing. Companies that were stable, large, and reliable for quality products and employment are under assault – or going out of business. Companies and services that did not even exist 10 years ago are now the largest, fastest-growing, and most profitable companies on the planet. For example, Amazon gets bigger while GM and GE are rushing to stay profitable and relevant.[1] How is this even possible?

1

So, we ask the question, what has happened to our economy and world? First, it has become global. You can build and sell your products nearly anywhere on the planet today. This was not true even a few decades ago. Today it is. Second, the world is rapidly becoming well-off enough to buy those products and services from anyone and anywhere in the world.[2] In the past, companies used to worry about competitors and customers in Indiana. Today, they are selling to and competing with customers and companies in India.

Everything has changed – and keeps changing faster than we can even imagine. Change is no longer incremental – it is exponential. The speed of change is one of the key differences in today's world. And that change is in every aspect of our lives. We often just want to yell "STOP" so we can get off the carousel. But, we can't. And, neither can anyone else.

If there is one thing that has occurred consistently, it is the speed and amount of change that is happening daily. If we can count on nothing else, it is the amount of change.

What has caused this change in our world and our economy? What has caused the change – and accelerates it daily – is the ability for anyone in the world to learn new ideas and apply them. Yes, at anytime and anywhere, a person can learn and do new things that before only a few would even know about and even fewer could actually do. Today, information availability and skillset development is unlimited – for everyone in the world. That is all 7 billion people alive today! Wow! That is mind blowing for most of us.

With the widespread ease of use of the internet, you can know just about anything from any place on the planet. And, you can begin to do it from just about any place as well. This changes everything we once knew about our economy. Also, technology can be obtained by anyone now. It is not just limited to those who have lots of money and resources. The cost, usefulness, and speed of technology has made it nearly accessible to everyone everywhere. These changes in the rules of today's economy make a lot of people, especially us Boomers, nervous and worried. It is not the world we grew up in. However, two generations did – Millennials and Gen Xers. (More about this later, but just know that they have something that the rest of us need.)

There are individuals, leaders, and companies thriving in this new economy. It is their lessons and their stories that I will share with you. The challenge is daunting. However, the solution exists for you to thrive just like they are. In this book, you will not only learn what you need to do, but you will learn how to do it.

It is critical that you learn how to thrive in the new economy. And, I believe nearly everyone can learn to thrive in it. However, those who do not could be left behind and miss out on what is in store. And I do not want that to happen. This new economy has the opportunity to be one of the most fair and diverse set of opportunities ever offered to the people on our planet.

Also, it is important that you not listen to the doomsday prophets who claim that jobs – including your job – will be replaced by artificial intelligence (AI) and robots.[3] This is just not true. In fact, what you will find out is that properly motivated and prepared individuals and companies will use both AI and robots to make their work, their lives, and the world around them better.[4] And, we will only grow to love our meaningful work more in the new economy which we will create in the future.

Fear in the workplace can be replaced with meaning, excellence, and success. This is the real story of the new economy. Get ready to be excited about what is to come. Once you know about it and how to thrive in it, you will be able to create a better future for you and those you care about.

Before we move on, let me share one of the critical attributes you will need to be successful in the new economy – perseverance. You will need to learn to change and persevere in order to thrive in our world today. Do not feel discouraged about this, because you can – and will – if only you know how to and take common sense actions. I know you can do it. Let's journey forward!

- 2 -

HOW TO USE THIS BOOK – AND CHANGE YOUR LIFE FOREVER

I want you to get the most out of this book. If you have read this far, you are ready to be successful. Congratulations - most people never even pick up a book to make their lives better. You have!

Now I will share the secret to lead a successful life. Why? Because I want – and need – you to be wildly successful. I am absolutely convinced that the change you need to bring to the world is waiting to be unleashed. And, the world badly needs it! The world needs changing – and you are the person for the job. Each of us is what the world needs now in our families, our organizations, our communities, and our world. If you do not bring it, it will not happen. That is why we need you to know how to be wildly successful. The success of the world depends on it.

You are unique and no one can do what you can do. No one is built the way you are to change the world in your way. We need you to do it. No one else can do it like you can.

I have designed this book so you can use it in whatever way you need to. This book is for you. This book is not about my life, rather it is about your life. I want you to have the life you want. I want you to be the leader you want to be. I want you to lead successful teams and organizations – the way only you can do so. We need you to be able to do that. Our world needs to change. You must become the change our world needs.

You can read this book in the order you want to. Each chapter of the book can stand on its own. Each chapter has stories, lessons, examples, takeaways, and practical habits. I think it makes more sense from front to back, but it is your book to use and your book to implement – any way you want. It's your life. It's your only life. I honor your ability to use it as you see fit. I only wish for you to have the fullest, most awesome life you can imagine!

Each chapter has a Practical Habit. This part of the chapter is important to helping you become a Present-Future Leader. It can help you be a better person and live a happier life. It will help you learn to be the person you always wanted to be – starting now.

I'm here to share with you how to begin to change your life right now. Yes, right now. Change is instantaneous. It can happen in seconds. Let me illustrate this for you. Think of one person you are grateful to have in your life. Just one. Smile and express gratitude for them. Right now. In less than 30 seconds you have put the habit of gratitude into your life. And, I bet it made you feel better. Trust me – if you use this habit every day, it will change your life for the better. Each morning I say a prayer of gratitude for the people I love the most in my life. I say their names and picture their faces. It takes me less than one minute. I put this habit into my life on December 26, 2015. As of this writing, I have done it every day since – that is over 750 days! I am a better person because of it. You can be, too.

THE HABIT-CREATION PROCESS IS AS FOLLOWS:

1. **Pick a habit** – the simpler, the better to start with.
2. **Do the habit** – immediately is best.
3. **Keep score that you did the habit** – find the method that works best for you, whether it be a smartphone app, a spreadsheet, or a notebook.
4. **Evaluate how you did** – what did you learn so you can improve?
5. **Repeat tomorrow** – and every day for the rest of your life!

That's it! You just changed your life - now keep it going. Later in this book, I will share more details on how you can develop your system for rapid and continuous change. Once you begin, you will get very good at changing your life. As you change your life, others will certainly notice. They too will follow your change leadership example. You will help the people you love the most first. Then, you will help the people you work with. You will help the people of your faith community, your local organizations, your region, your country, and even the world. That is how the world is changed – one person doing a courageous act of change one day at a time. Yes, be the change you want to see in the world – and you will see the change in the world you desire!

- 3 -

THE FOURTH INDUSTRIAL
REVOLUTION (OR INDUSTRY 4.0)

What is the Fourth Industrial Revolution or Industry 4.0? It is how historians and futurists are describing what is transpiring in manufacturing and technology today. We are all aware of the Industrial Revolution, however, to be accurate, there has been more than one.

Klaus Schwab, Founder and Executive Chairman of the World Economic Forum in Geneva, does an excellent job laying out the distinct elements of the four industrial revolutions:

The First Industrial Revolution (roughly 1760-1840) used water and steam power to mechanize production. The Second Industrial Revolution (roughly 1870-1914) used electric power to create mass production. The Third Industrial Revolution (roughly 1950-1970) used electronics and information technology to automate production. Now a Fourth Industrial Revolution is building on the Third. It is characterized by the fusion of technologies that merge the physical, digital, and biological spheres.[5]

The current revolution, Industry 4.0, has arrived with such speed and scope that it is disrupting every industry globally. We are confronted with fundamental changes in the way we live, work, and relate to one another.

Just some of the important changes I am seeing today at our member companies include:

- **Robots Assisting in Production**: Many of MACNY's members already have robot-assisted production working side-by-side with their current team members. Increasingly these robots are small, inexpensive, and are taking over repetitive, monotonous work.

- **Self-Driving Vehicles**: We have members at MACNY that have self-driving forklifts and self-driving parts delivery systems. This trend will only accelerate.

- **Production Line Simulations and Layouts**: Members use 3-D technology to simulate production lines before creating them. Production line redesign and deployment using simulation saves money and allows for better utilization of critical staff skills.

- **Smart Predictive Maintenance:** Smart devices in facilities today allow our members to predict failures. In the future, smart machines will likely independently maintain themselves.

- **Machines Sold as a Service**: Today, our manufacturing members sell a machine as a service. Instead of selling the entire machine to one of their customers, they set-up the machine, maintain it, and allow their customer to take full advantage of the services it provides.

The Boston Consulting Group (BCG), in its analysis of the impacts of Industry 4.0, tells us that:

We will see sensors, machines, workplaces, and IT systems that are connected along the value chain beyond a single enterprise. These connected systems can and will interact with one another using standard Internet-based protocols and will analyze data to predict failure, configure themselves, and adapt to changes. Industry 4.0 will make it possible to gather and analyze data across machines; enabling faster, more flexible, and more efficient processes to produce higher-quality goods at reduced costs. This in turn, will increase manufacturing productivity, shift economics, foster industrial growth, and modify the profile of the workforce. Ultimately, changing the competitiveness of companies and regions.[6]

What is becoming evident is that for technological advances to be implemented and to drive company success, the right people must be selected and trained to succeed in our new Industry 4.0 world. These skilled workers are in short supply. Companies will increasingly have to "grow their own." The Boston Consulting Group studied the status of adoption in two countries - Germany and the United States. Its study surveyed more than 600 managers and senior executives representing 312 German companies and 315 U.S. companies. They found that companies in both countries have been implementing Industry 4.0 technologies at about the same pace and that companies see the lack of qualified employees as their biggest challenge in implementing Industry 4.0.[7]

Industry 4.0 and the technologies involved are transforming our world. Gaining an understanding of the technologies and having a plan to upgrade our own skills and the skills of our employees will be critical to success in the 21st Century and beyond.

TAKEAWAYS:
1. The Fourth Industrial Revolution (Industry 4.0) will change everything you know about our economy.
2. Skilled workers are in short supply. If you are ready, you can thrive in our new economy driven by Industry 4.0 (the Fourth Industrial Revolution).

Practical Habit:
Beginning today, establish an effort to learn as much as you can about the Fourth Industrial Revolution (Industry 4.0). Use a variety of resources to become aware of what is transpiring to change today's economy.

- 4 -

PAST-PRESENT LEADERSHIP VS. PRESENT-FUTURE LEADERSHIP

I learned Past-Present Leadership from some very amazing leaders. They were what you might call Servant Leaders. They were serving their country and their units in the U.S. Army. They led from the front and were committed and brave. They would put their lives on the line – literally. Early in my Army career, many of my senior leaders were war veterans. Wisdom and, at times, a deep sadness was a part of how they led. Very few war veterans ever talked to me about their war experiences. Many had lost friends and colleagues in the effort. "War is hell" as one veteran told me – and no one wants to live in hell. But, their courage and strength had sustained them. It was easy to follow them out of respect and admiration.

Past-Present Leaders can give you the best of their wisdom and experience. They know what works because they have lived it. It's proven, it's tested, and it works for those involved. Rules and procedures are critical in a Past-Present Leadership environment. Standards must be established – and followed. Successful repetition and precision are needed. When I started my position at MACNY, this was so very evident. Factories need consistency and high-quality outcomes. Products must be uniform and work every time. GE went so far to insist on Six Sigma Quality.[8] Quality at the Six Sigma level is so high that only one part in a million is not to specifications. That is very high in quality.

Past-Present Leaders are hyper-focused on learning the lessons from past successes and failures. In the Army, every exercise was followed by an After Action Review (AAR). We were keen on learning from the past and improving for the future. The past was the Holy Grail of future success. This was true of nearly every successful organization I was in after I left the Army. A learning pattern from the past was embedded in every process and outcome. We learned from the past so we could be more successful in the future. In the past, market disruption was rare. Existing organizations and companies who held significant mind space and market share dominated for decades. Companies just needed to incrementally improve to dominate the present—or so they thought. "If it isn't broke, don't fix it" was a common mantra. We lived by it as Past-Present Leaders.

Past-Present Leaders have a large degree of confidence that tomorrow's economy and organizational situations will be very much like today. We can keep doing what we do – getting a little better – because what is working today will work tomorrow. This makes a lot of sense when the day-to-day is changing at a predictable

14

rate. It makes a lot of sense when what you did yesterday will be successful today. But, what happens when tomorrow and tomorrow's tomorrow are going to be very different? What happens when new technology, new ideas, and new competitors are emerging rapidly? Can what we did yesterday and today be enough to keep us competitive? Increasingly, the answer is no. Leaders must now focus on what the future looks like so they can rapidly lead their organizations towards it. Past-Present Leaders need to adapt who they are to become Present-Future Leaders so they can thrive in today's global and rapidly changing world.

WHY IS THE PAST IMPORTANT?

It is critical that leaders pay attention to the past. In our past, and in the past of our organizations, lie important lessons and memories that can guide our present and future. However, it can also constrain us if we let it. In my experience, an organization that holds on tightly to the past does not focus on inventing their successful futures. The past becomes a trap that prohibits forward motion.

The past is a treasure of lessons learned. No organization or person gets to be successful without a meaningful and productive past. It is how you got here. However, what got you here won't take you into the future. It can only set the stage for it. A Present-Future Leader can honor and learn from the past. They must. But, they cannot become a hostage to it.

If we are genuine in honoring the past, it sets the stage for change. Honoring the past is about honoring the leaders of successful organizations. At MACNY, we have a Wall of Fame. Each year at our Annual Dinner we select two additional legendary leaders to grace our Wall of Fame. This Wall of Fame is the most prominent feature of our office. On it are some of the legends that have built our community by building their companies into amazing success stories. Some are also community leaders. It is a moving experience to honor these individuals and their companies. When we honor the people for what they have done we celebrate the past in an appropriate way.

Our Wall of Fame is not a wall of companies. It is a wall of people because these are leaders who show the way to future success. Successful organizations are led by successful people. These companies will continue to change and adapt to remain successful. New leaders will be responsible for seeing that through. No company can stay the same doing what it did in the past. It must create the future. Present-Future Leaders have the capacity to do this well.

Great leaders honor the past, and the people who made it possible, while charting a path to a successful future. Without such leaders, our companies and communities falter. I know because I have seen this while serving the members of MACNY.

How Does A Leader Transition To Present-Future Leadership While Honoring The Past?

We know that the past is important and cannot be discarded. We also now know that individuals and organizations must rapidly change to be successful in the future. How can we account for these important truths while moving forward? We must fully live in the present with our efforts focused on creating the future. The past is truly a part of the present. Organizations and individuals are the result of their past experiences and choices. What has worked in the past is what is carried forward to today. We can honor the past when we acknowledge the people and the processes that have survived the test of time. We also honor the past when we do what we must do to ensure business thrives into the future. Change is inevitable in today's economy and world and that change must occur faster than ever.

Today's successful leaders must be firmly rooted in the present with a laser like focus on how to get to a successful future. And, that is what I will turn my attention to in the next section.

TAKEAWAYS:

1. Past-Present Leaders focus on what worked in the past and continue to apply it today. The past offers important lessons to help us with our efforts.

2. Present-Future Leaders know they must build on the past but focus on the future. Each day is a day to implement what must be achieved to be viable in the future.

PRACTICAL HABIT:

Assess your current focus and activity. Is it primarily focused on what you did in the past? In what ways can you begin to do new activities that help you better implement the future starting today?

- 5 -

BECOMING A
PRESENT-FUTURE LEADER

The current economic situation requires us to act and lead differently. The old way of leading – practiced by Past-Present leaders, will no longer work. Our economy is littered with companies and individuals who have tried to maintain this approach. They stayed stuck in the past, doing what used to work, and then went out of business – quickly or very slowly. Regardless of speed, the result was the same.

The new successful leader is the Present-Future Leader. This leader is well equipped to not only survive, but thrive in our new global economy. So, what does this successful Present-Future Leader look like?

Present-Future Leaders are different from Past-Present Leaders in many significant ways. The biggest difference is that Present-Future leaders are always focused on how they are developing into the leaders they need to be and they are leading their organizations into an exciting, meaningful, and compelling future. Past-

Present Leaders are mostly concerned about maintaining past successes. This is true in their own lives as well as in the lives of those they work with. How do I know this difference? I see it in my own life and in the lives of many company leaders. However, that is rapidly changing. I see the future of leadership emerging each day. These are the leaders I see adapting and becoming Present-Future Leaders.

So, what does becoming a Present-Future Leader look like? The first thing I notice, and you can to, is these leaders are full of passion and excitement—and the people around them are too. You might even call it joy. In fact, it seems infectious. People seem to smile a lot – and like each other. They are incredibly productive because they are focused, often autonomous or team-led, and producing remarkable outcomes. Yes, they even seem to be having fun! I remember my first experience with this kind of leader and this kind of Present-Future Company. I will never forget it.

I had just gotten my new job at MACNY, The Manufacturers Association, and was invited out to an incredible company called Welch Allyn for a personal visit with Bill Allyn, the President and CEO at the time. It was quite an honor. He, and his company, are legendary in the Syracuse area and I had a chance to meet him personally and visit the iconic company. I'll never forget how friendly he was to me. He greeted me with a huge smile and a welcome fit for someone he had known for years. To this day, it makes me smile when I think about it. We spent a few minutes chatting and then he excitedly offered to give me a tour of the company. We walked down to the production floor – a high-tech workspace making some of the most sophisticated medical instruments anywhere in the world. As we walked the floor, he greeted everyone by name and asked about their families and how they were – he was clearly genuine and cared deeply about them. He knew more than just their names – he knew their lives. I noticed immediately that he was not the "boss," he was their friend and leader. He knew each part of the facility inside and out. I am not sure who was more excited to see it – him or me. He was like a kid in a candy shop. He was truly enjoying the entire experience. This was not just his work – it was his life. It gave meaning to everything he did. He had built this company with the people who worked there. He grasped both the history of the organization and its future. It was special. And, it was my first exposure to what a Present-Future Leader was like – I just did not know it at the time.

Your first experience with a Present-Future Leader will also leave a lasting impression. Why? Because you will want to work there too!

Bill Allyn gave me a glimpse of the future 16 years ago. I have spent the last five years gaining a greater understanding of what is needed to become such a person. I have undertaken my own journey to become a Present-Future Leader. I have witnessed many others who have undergone this change – and those who have not – now I am going to share this with you. Also, I am going to guide you on your own journey to become this

21

kind of leader and how to thrive in today's economy. Are you ready!? Let's get started.

TAKEAWAYS:

1. The current economy requires us to lead different. We must be focused on creating the future each day.
2. Present-Future Leaders create environments that reflect their demonstrated actions – workplaces full of passion, excitement, and achievement. People enjoy working there – you see them smile a lot - and they are incredibly productive.

PRACTICAL HABIT:

Take note of workplaces where the environment encourages high levels of commitment, passion, excitement, and achievement. Identify why you think that is so – and look to emulate that behavior in your own life.

- 6 -

THE FUTURE IS NOW!

SEE AND EXPERIENCE THE FUTURE NOW

To be a Present-Future Leader you must be able to understand the future. You may be wondering how that is possible. I'm here to tell you that the future already exists – it is just not widely distributed.

In my role as President and CEO of MACNY I get to see the future every time I visit a technology company. They are using the latest in both technology and management strategies. Other organizations I visit are sometimes behind in both. When you are in a globally competitive industry you cannot afford to lag behind because if you do, you could go out of business quickly. The speed of business change today almost guarantees it. This means that technology companies are often living the future first. Therefore, if you want to see the future you only need to know where to look. And, with the internet, it's even easier to find—thanks, Google!

Go ahead – try it. Google the topic of robotics. You will find page after page of the latest uses of robotics that could transform your business into the future. How about implementing lean practices or using Six Sigma? Yup. There are endless resources being used by cutting edge companies around the globe.

Last year, I took a cruise down the Danube with my wife, my parents, my brother and his wife, and some friends. One of the excursions offered was a trip to the BMW factory in Germany. An entire bus of interested travelers on the cruise traveled to the plant. At this facility, each car is different and unique. For instance, you can have any color you want. One woman brought her favorite nail polish color to the dealer and that is what she got. There are also 12,000 different variations of seat designs. The list of options goes on and on. Every one of the 1,300 cars that roll off the line each day is unique and different. Ten thousand people work there along with the most technologically advanced robots in the world. It cost me all of $130 to see the amazing future of manufacturing.[9]

Everyone on the tour saw the future that day. This was not possible even a decade ago. So, the future is there for the enterprising individual, leader, and company to readily understand and begin to use. Before leaders had to look to the past to see what worked. Now leaders must look to the future so they can transform their businesses. And don't for a second think you need to witness all of these amazing tours in person, a video can be just as effective.

24

Of course, not everything that is happening is the future. Some of what is happening will pass away or be changed to better reflect what will work in the future. Also, implementing the future is a process that changes each day as you bring the future into your workplace. This is what makes Present-Future Leaders so valuable. They not only have to help their businesses identify what is rapidly being created, they have to know how to introduce it into the present of their current organization. A good way to do this is to begin working with the workforce of the future – Millennials.

MILLENNIALS ARE THE SOLUTION

For a long-time I heard from leaders of companies that they did not understand the new employees of their companies. They were "different," "unmotivated," "entitled," and "always on their phones." These were some of the kinder complaints. Baby Boomers are retiring and leaders are genuinely concerned that the next generation is not up to the task of replacing them. They want a "solution" to change the ways of the up-and-coming workforce.

Today I tell company leaders, if you want to see the future workforce, spend time with Millennials. The way they work and solve problems is your solution! They are not the problem - they are your only solution to remaining competitive. In fact, I go so far as to say that I want to "grow up" to be like them!

The way I see it, the Millennials are my kids. I have three twenty-something year old daughters. They are smart, tech savvy, kind, tolerant, and hard-working individuals. They were raised to do what they love and to believe they could do anything they set their minds to. One is a mechanical engineer, one is an industrial designer, and the youngest is currently a college student studying business. With their educations and talents, they will certainly do more and go further than me. That's what I – and lots of parents – hope for. However, they work differently. Leaders must begin to use the unique talents and capabilities of Millennials to thrive in our world. Did you know that 10,000 Baby Boomers (born from 1946-1964) retire each day in America? [10] Did you know that by 2020 Millennials (born from 1982-2002) will make up 65% of the workforce? How about the fact that there are just not enough Gen Xers (born from 1965-1981) to move into Boomer jobs and roles in organizations?[11] All of these facts point to an undeniable conclusion – Millennials are the future of your workforce. Isn't it time to transition to a workplace where they can be most productive and help your company thrive? I certainly think so.

In the workplace, it is more vital than ever to begin a multi-generation conversation. Boomers need to talk to both Gen Xers and Millennials. A leader needs to understand the expectations of each generation within their workplace. In many organizations, a mix of all three generations leads to a culture that is setting the tone for how a leader leads into the future.

TAKEAWAYS:

1. We can all experience the future today. We can see it when we visit existing organizations and on the internet. The future does exist already – it is just not widely distributed.

2. Millennials are the future workforce and offer us the opportunity to learn what the workplace of the future will look like. This will all occur very soon since so many Boomers are retiring and leaving the workforce.

PRACTICAL HABIT:

If you are a Boomer or Gen Xer, spend time with Millennials starting today. If you are a Millennial, build relationships with the other generations so they can understand what you bring to the workplace today that helps the company be more successful.

- 7 -

IT MUST HAVE MEANING!

Can everything we do have meaning? I believe it can – for most things. If what we are asked to do is immoral or illegal, then probably not. Just about everything else could qualify. Let me give you an example – candles.

I love the smell of candles. One place that candles serve an important purpose is in our places of worship. In many churches, you will find sacramental candles that occupy a prominent place on the altar. They are for special purposes like a Paschal Candle in the Catholic Church that is lit each Sunday beginning with Easter.

Candles are an ancient product that have primarily been relegated to low cost labor countries. However, there is a wonderful candle making company (and MACNY member) in Syracuse, New York by the name of Cathedral Candle Company. It is a family-owned business led by two brothers, Mark and Louis Steigerwald, who are some of the nicest people I've ever met. Now, you may be saying, "so what is so noble about making candles?" And, my answer is "the Pope."

Yes, Cathedral Candle Company makes candles for the Pope in Rome. The Pope of the Roman Catholic Church is the leader of over one billion people. And, candles made right here in Syracuse, NY are used during the Masses that the Pope says in Rome, Italy. If you happen to be a person of faith, that is very inspiring. Thus, as you might imagine, they have a very powerful "why." If that is not enough, they also make candles for many, many churches throughout the world. Cathedral Candle Company produces one of the highest quality candles anywhere and they burn in nothing less than a spectacular way. I absolutely love to visit them and their factory. The Steigerwald brothers are Present-Future Leaders with a very powerful "why." And, by the way, they are quite successful.

There was a time when work was just "work." Employees were expected to give a day's work for a day's pay. Employees were instructed on what to do – and they did it as a condition of employment. Well, those days are just about over. In today's economy, our work must have meaning or employees will either underperform or leave. But, employers cannot exist long if they continue to lose their employees. Turnover is costly and will ultimately kill a company. So, what has changed?

Today's incoming workers – millennials – want their work to have meaning. You really do need to start with "why," as Simon Sinek says.[12] A compelling why is absolutely critical to getting millennials, and increasingly all workers, to give one hundred percent of their talent.

As a team member, you must also find your why. It is no longer feasible for any of us to just go to work each day to collect a paycheck—we need to be passionate about what we do. Defining our "why" is how we find our passion. Passion is the key to our success. When we are excited and committed to something we give it all we've got—and then some. And in order for us to be outstanding at what we do, we must give all we have to the effort. If we don't, someone else will and they will be the ones who are successful. So, for our own success, what we do must have meaning to us.

TAKEAWAYS:

1. It is critical that you be explicit about your "why" and your company's "why." Millennials, and increasingly all generations, want to work for a company with a compelling purpose and mission. Present-Future Leaders have a compelling "why."

2. Become passionate about your "why" and your company's "why." It is critical to success!

PRACTICAL HABIT:

Develop your why. Write it down. Make sure it is consistent with your company's mission and purpose. It's what will set you apart as a Present-Future Leader. Once you've written it down, be sure to share it with others, including your team members.

- 8 -

Is It Getting Done?

Nearly every business and organization needs to re-invent itself to remain vibrant and profitable. I have witnessed such re-creations time and time again in MACNY Member companies. This does not mean a company must give up its core business or its past successes. It does mean it must reinvent how it does business and reaches new customers. Welch Allyn made basic physician equipment early in its organizational history and today makes sophisticated hospital diagnostic equipment. Corning was known for its homeware and today makes Gorilla® Glass for smartphones. Stickley started as a craft furniture maker and today makes world-famous furnishings for all aspects of your home and office in a variety of styles. Giovanni Foods once made simple sauces for a limited clientele and today is a custom producer of a variety of products that you can find in major grocery retailers across the country. Time and time again I have seen companies become even more successful by reinventing their products and business.

There has never been a time when getting it done has become so important. When the world, the economy, and your business are changing this fast, no leader can afford to not accomplish meaningful outcomes. It also has become even easier to get distracted by useless activity. In fact, with all the digital devices we have, we can be busier than ever and get almost nothing of meaning done. So, let's get specific – you and your business must achieve important outcomes and that means getting the most meaningful tasks completed each day—even when other things try to get in the way.

I believe it is important right up front to accept that distractions are often the number one reason why leaders, their teams, and organizations do not get what is important done. We get sidetracked into activity that does not support our mission. We can be constantly bombarded by e-mails, texts, calls, and dozens of notifications from our smartphones that we spend almost no time working on the deep, meaningful, and innovative work we must do to be personally and organizationally successful. Acknowledging, identifying, and finally minimizing distractions is critical to getting what we need done actually done.

We also need to get clear on what needs to be done. Do you know what is critical? Do you write it down and constantly refer to it? Does your team know what needs to get done? Are they committed to it? One of the reasons why distractions can take up so much of our time is we may not be clear on our priorities. Knowing what must get done must come first!

As we clear away distractions and become hyper-focused on what is meaningful, we have to schedule it and commit to doing it – fast. Speed of implementation is the key to our ultimate success. For instance, there is a lot of talk about minimum viable product these days - and rightfully so. Speed to implementation means we need to get a product to our customers so they can help us decide if it is viable and how we can improve it. The same can be said of our services. We need to offer services and test how effectively we are providing them. Then we can change our products and services to better fit the need of our customers so our sales will increase.

We also need to keep score to ensure it is getting done. I will discuss this in detail later, but suffice to say that we must be committed to getting it done in order for us even to care about keeping score.

I have also found that both as a leader and a team member, we are confronted by colleagues who are not committed to getting meaningful work done. In today's world, it is not acceptable to stand still. We must get meaningful work done or we will go out of business. So, we must address issues that stand in the way of us focusing on what must be done. What makes this so critical today is that the speed of change is accelerating and the longer we fail to focus and achieve outcomes the further behind we find ourselves.

One of the key strategies to getting others to care about getting meaningful work done is to share your own reasons and passion. When someone does not understand why or lacks passion for it, they can be moved by your why and passion. My why and passion, especially as a leader, can make all the difference in the world. It is often the spark needed to get the ball rolling to accomplishing great things.

As with companies, leaders need to reinvent themselves. Any leader that stays the same will become obsolete. I can say that I have completely renewed my leadership style and continue to transform it each day and each year. I have been blessed to lead MACNY since 2001. The way I led in the beginning of my tenure and how I lead now are remarkably different. I needed to become a Present-Future Leader much like my member companies needed to become Present-Future Organizations led by Present-Future Leaders who are recreating their own leadership approaches to reflect much more than the past. They needed to seek the future with a conviction and resoluteness that transforms systems – and especially the people who work in these amazing organizations.

TAKEAWAYS:

1. It has never been more important to get your important tasks as a leader and as organizations done. We must constantly ask ourselves - "is it getting done?"

2. Sharing your passion and reasons for getting important work done will help overcome resistance to change within your organization.

PRACTICAL HABIT:

Reinvention of a company starts with its leader. Create a list of ways in which you are reinventing yourself in the coming year. I do this on an annual basis so that I can change as my organization is changing. An annual leadership change plan makes a very big difference!

- 9 -

MOVE QUICKLY AND
KEEP MOVING!

When I first arrived at MACNY, we were offering what we had traditionally provided to members. I could see that we needed to create more value for members within our traditional offerings. I could also see we needed to bring new offerings to members. Moving as quickly as staff and members would allow was the key to creating both additional value and growth in our offerings and revenues. There were plenty of adjustments to make. Some new efforts needed to be modified. Some did not work as planned. But, in the end, we created a different organization that built on our tradition while offering many new services. MACNY's successful manufacturing members do this as well. Building upon their traditional products, they've continued to offer new products using existing capabilities and, as needed, they've add new capabilities. As you can imagine, sitting still is how leaders, and their organizations, fall behind.

The successful Present-Future Leader is known for moving quickly. If we are to compete successfully and thrive, we need to evolve and remain relevant. An organization and a leader cannot do this without rapid change. I have seen the difference between leaders and organizations that move quickly toward the future and those that linger in the past. If an organization moves too slowly, the competition – or even new competitors – will overtake them. This can happen quickly, much to many leaders' surprise.

One of the key capacities a leader must develop is the ability to change rhythm or pace. Our teams need to know that we are moving toward the future as quickly as we can. Every aspect of our businesses will need to be recreated. Our products and services must be improved and expanded. There is no one pace for such activity – other than quickly. A leader needs to develop a strategic direction, an implementation plan, project teams, and defined timelines and outcomes. Racing to the future must become a way of life. How fast depends on the business market and the organization's team members.

Of course, change can become too fast and overwhelming. I recommend leaders temporarily slow down, but remain moving. Relentless change is needed – how fast can be regulated. What I have seen is that team members are the ones who know how fast the organization can go. A leader listening to their team can regulate speed of change – increasing and moderating as needed to be successful. Listen to your team members and they will help set a sustainable path forward.

What gets in the way of moving quickly is indecision. When we stop completely or abandon our commitment to change we are doomed to fail. Change is no longer optional, it's inevitable. The only option is the speed at which to change.

The best change is driven by strategic focus and specific outcomes. This is where a leader needs to be decisive. How often is your strategic plan revisited? How much does it need to be updated? Does your strategic plan need a complete overhaul? Strategic planning conversations should occur at least annually. Updates should be even more frequent so that the plan and efforts stay relevant.

It is as important to keep moving on creating future opportunities. Movement is the key to success. Quick pilots and turn-around are needed. And, it must all be done with quality in mind. Moving into the future requires these boundaries or else worthwhile action will be primarily focused on maintaining the status quo. Change is not easy. However, when an organization expects and wants to change, the equation shifts. Resistance to change must shift to desire for improvement and success.

TAKEAWAYS:

1. Present-Future Leaders must move quickly and keep moving.
2. Develop a change rhythm as a leader. Modify it as the situation demands – but do not stop moving forward into the future.

PRACTICAL HABIT:

Create a strategic planning routine for yourself as a leader and for your organization. Routinely review it, potentially even daily, to ensure you stay true to your strategic direction and can move as quickly as you can.

- 10 -

IT'S DECISION TIME!

Joe Vargo is a talented community leader and the Executive Director of a 25-year-old community organization that helps approximately 7,000 students and teachers experience career pathways each year. However, during the Great Recession, Partners for Education & Business (PEB) was struggling financially. Joe asked for a meeting with me to discuss the future. Continuing on PEB's current path was one fraught with great risk. Changing course was also tough to envision. As we sat and talked about what a joint MACNY and PEB future might look like, we both got excited, yet we were not sure how to execute it. There was not a clear model for this kind of joint organization. It was decision time – and we both knew it.

As an individual and as a leader, you will need to make decisions, or else they will be made for you. Not deciding is a decision. So, each day you will be offered a choice to do it the way you have done it – or change the way you are doing it to better reflect the future. This is the fundamental difference between Past-Present Leaders and Present-Future Leaders. It's a decision to live in the present executing actions that lead to a brighter future. In today's fast-paced world, we get to choose. Choose wisely – it will matter a lot to you and your organization.

Every leader and person gets to live in the present. It really is all we have. However, a fundamental difference I see in leaders is how they are focused. For successful businesses to continue to create value and thrive, they must be future focused. They cannot only be doing what worked in the past – they must increasingly work on what is needed in the future. Each day becomes a decision to seek what the future will be like and begin to create what is necessary to thrive tomorrow. We must make a series of decisions to live today that enable us to both serve existing customers and create what will serve future customers. Practical research and development of the path to the future must take up more and more of a leader's time. Being good at what we now do is foundation to survive. Being good at what is needed by our customers and clients in the future is how we get ahead and truly grow as both individuals and companies.

Of course, you will have doubts. They are inevitable. Others will doubt as well. But, you must grapple with your doubts and continue your forward leaning efforts. Dive into your doubts and those of others. What is at the heart of the doubts? Is it fear? Are there specific barriers? Can you still proceed, but differently? If you must change – and you must continue to change – then dealing with your doubts and fears are a part of being a leader. If you show humility in your search for answers, care deeply about others, and want to desperately serve your customers; then you will very likely find the path forward. In fact, it will be the challenges that help define what will work and move a good idea to a successful business product or service.

Make no mistake about it, it is decision time. You will need to step up your game to be successful in a global, demanding, and ever-changing world. But, to not decide is in itself a decision. Successful leaders and individuals know this. And once they decide, they can begin to become the leaders and team players that our successful businesses and organizations so desperately need today.

In 2010, Joe and I decided to move forward and make PEB an affiliate of MACNY. We sought financial help from the Central New York Community Foundation. We got our respective board chairs and Executive Committees involved. We crafted a plan of action – and changed it as needed. We had to – nowhere else in the nation did we have a model to work off. However, it worked well – even better than we had planned. We secured the future of our two organizations and are creating the workforce of the future. The opportunities we have had have soared over the last eight years. All because we were willing to make a decision for the future – and act upon it!

TAKEAWAYS:

1. You are making a decision when you don't decide. So, go ahead and make the best decision possible as soon as possible.
2. Choose the future – even when it is unclear. You will learn as you create the future.

PRACTICAL HABIT:

You must practice making decisions that choose the future over the present. Decisive decision- making is a necessary habit of the Present-Future Leader. What is the one decision you need to make today? Make it! And, repeat tomorrow!

- 11 -

LEADERSHIP WISDOM

Lieutenant Colonel (LTC) Belich was one of my first commanders when I was in the Army. I was a relatively new lieutenant and assigned to the 3-17 Cavalry Squadron as a part of an initial team of five officers. It was our task to build, from scratch, a new helicopter scout unit to support the 10th Mountain Division's Light Infantry Brigades. Over the next year, we needed to receive all of the other soldiers and the Squadron's heavy equipment and prepare the unit for combat. We would write all of the Standard Operating Procedures (SOPs) and go through rigorous combat training. In the end, the unit would be tested at the National Training Center (NTC) in Ft. Irwin, California. It was an exhilarating experience that tested everyone in the unit. Leading this effort was LTC Belich, a Vietnam War veteran and seasoned officer. For me LTC Belich was the embodiment of leadership wisdom. He used the past to understand what the future needed to look like for the unit. He was inspired by our mission – and inspired us. He always wanted us to strive for more and yet could compliment us on our efforts so far. He saw leadership as a professional journey not an ultimate destination. He learned with me even though he was so much more experienced than me. He left a lasting impression on me.

We have all met that leader that has impressed us with how they seem to effortlessly inspire and lead others. They just have a way of getting others to go above and beyond the call of duty. I have met plenty of such leaders over the years of my professional journey. What they have is what I like to call Leadership Wisdom.

So, what is leadership wisdom? And, how do we get it as leaders? I believe that leadership wisdom is the result of a lifetime commitment to becoming a leader with integrity who serves a cause greater than oneself. It's a journey that is both humbling and exhilarating. It includes the highs of success and the lows of failure. And, the good ones never reach the destination but always remain open and devoted learners of their craft.

In today's world, we need strong leaders more than ever. We need them to solve difficult global and local problems. We need them to grow our economy in a sustainable way. We need them in our homes, our places of worship, our communities, and in our nation's capital. However, I find myself wondering, will we have enough to tackle all of our needs?

I fundamentally believe that we are all called to lead – in some small or large way. I believe we can all discover and develop leadership wisdom. But, we will not do it alone and in isolation. We will primarily discover it in others – in order to develop in ourselves. It is why I decided to attend the United States Military Academy at West Point. I wanted to become a leader while serving my country.

While there, and later in the Army, I learned that leaders are made and not born. And, it is primarily modeled and achieved through the life-long discovery of doing what matters as we develop habits that allow us to excel in our moments of decision. Also, it usually shows itself in times of trial and hardship. I find it easy to lead when things are going well. It is much harder – but more rewarding – in times of challenge.

So, how can you gain leadership wisdom? Identify and learn from great and wise leaders. Become a life-long learner. With today's internet, you can read about modern day leaders and those in the past. You can watch videos and movies. You can also meet them in your own communities or anywhere in the world – in person or virtually. You can be inspired and captivated by how they lead. When someone inspires you – it is usually a good sign that they can teach you how to lead wisely. My friend Adolphe Nyakasane is just such a leader.

I met Adolphe while he was participating in a Young African Leaders Program in 2016. He invited me to coffee at my alma mater, Syracuse University, where the program was being held. He is a pediatrician in the Democratic Republic of the Congo. But, he is so much more. He is a community leader who leads a vibrant nonprofit to help children and their families overcome poverty and malnutrition. Today, he is my hero. If you meet him, I am quite certain you would agree.

What makes Adolphe so impressive is his passion for change and his gentle compassion for those in significant need. Through will and prayer he leads in whatever way is called for. He listens, learns, and inspires. He is brilliant – and yet humble. And, his smile will light up your face with the love he holds for you and others.

Adolphe is wise beyond his years. Through the struggles to care for the most vulnerable in the Congo, where malnutrition can impact 50% of children, he has found leadership wisdom. It is my pleasure to work with him and learn leadership wisdom from him even though we are thousands of miles apart. Through the magic of Skype and the Internet, we have stayed close and connected. Once you find a friend who is a truly wise leader – connect and learn from them frequently. It will change who you are as a leader – and as a person.

TAKEAWAYS:

1. Leadership Wisdom is developed over time and often by practicing what other leaders who inspire us have modeled.
2. We do not become wise on our own or by just reading about it. We develop leadership wisdom by practicing it and learning from others.

PRACTICAL HABIT:

Identify one or more leaders who inspire you. What is one habit or tendency they have? Begin to use it daily in your own life. After you do one, pick another – and another. Over time you will become wiser and more effective.

To learn more about my friend Adolphe Nyakasane and the amazing work he does, visit:
http://www.keshokongo.org/

- 12 -

BE TRULY PRESENT

Have you ever been to a steel plant? It is truly an amazing experience. The melting metals and the large machines take you back to a different era. Crucible Industries is just that. Jim Beckman is the former President of Crucible Industries and former chair of MACNY's Board of Directors. More importantly to me, he is a wonderfully kind person and friend of mine. When Jim is with you he is truly present with you. No phone interrupts your time with him. He is not busy looking to do other things. He wants to know how he can help. He is genuine in his concern. Jim brought Crucible Industries, a company that is over 100 years old, through the Great Recession. He saved the company and hundreds of jobs by leading them through bankruptcy and back to profitability - no small task. He is beloved by the team at Crucible Industries and he is beloved at MACNY. One of the reasons is because he is fully present to those he is with.

One of the key characteristics of great leaders is their ability to live in the present. The mind tends to spend its time in the past or in the future. However, you cannot get anything done in the past or the future – only in the now. When leaders are fully present in the now, they can have the maximum impact on their lives and the lives of others. When a person is fully present they are listening, learning, and interacting with those around them.

We know when someone is fully present to us. They look at us and pay attention. They respond to our cues for feedback and interaction. They connect with us. Others know when we are fully present with them when we use the same behaviors. In today's world of distraction, this has become so very difficult to do – but it has never been more important. People respond to leaders who are there for them. Team members follow a leader who knows them and cares for them and wants to accomplish meaningful outcomes. When you are present, you can do these things. When you are not, it shows – and your effectiveness as a leader diminishes.

To be truly present, we have to slow ourselves down and listen to the other person. Do we hear them? Do we understand them? Do they know we are listening and caring and striving to help them be successful in accomplishing their mission? These are all important questions to ask ourselves as we are living and leading in the present.

Living in the present also has real effectiveness benefits. When we are present we can stay focused. We can get things done. If our minds drift to the past or future, we get distracted which makes us less productive. This is why most multitasking fails. Neuroscientists tell us we do not really multitask as humans. We switch task. And, switch tasking is inherently less effective – and less efficient. It is especially so when we are with others. It sends a strong message that the tasks we are switching to are more important than the person we are with. This lowers our ability to be effective with them. So, focus intently on one task at a time and execute it well – especially if that task involves work with others. They are so critical to your success and the organization's success.

TAKEAWAYS:

1. Great leaders are truly present. They listen, learn, and care about others.
2. We cannot effectively multitask – we switch task. When we are multitasking with people we are not fully present to them and we miss our chance to connect and lead well.

PRACTICAL HABIT:

Practice putting away any distractions and tasks while you are with others. It will clear your mind and make you more effective.

- 13 -

PASSION IS KEY!

If you do not have passion for your future, it will not happen. I didn't always believe this. I do now. To be a Present-Future Leader you must be passionate about what you are accomplishing. Without it, you will likely stay in the present and quickly reflect upon the past wondering how the world passed you by. Let me tell you about my friend Nate Andrews. Nate Andrews is the President of Morse Manufacturing. Nate is a third-generation leader of a small manufacturer that makes industrial drum handling equipment that is sold around the world. Everything I see Nate do is done with such passion! He is a husband, father, community leader, competitive swimmer, and Present-Future Leader in manufacturing. It's not easy leading a small manufacturing company into the future with world-wide competitors. One such competitor in China even reverse engineered Morse's product and then attempted to sell it - with the Morse name on it! Others have been less blatant in stealing their designs - but have copied their success just the same. How does Morse do more than survive? It starts with passionate leadership.

DOES GREAT LEADERSHIP REQUIRE PASSION?

I believe that great leadership most certainly requires passion. I have found it requires a passion for the mission and a passion for the people who undertake the mission. And, in my experience, they are both required to be successful and sustainable. Passion for people and mission allow us to create the future of our organizations. To find our passion, we usually need to start with our "why" – why are we doing what we are doing? Have you identified your why?

Passion for the mission is necessary to focus a leader on what is to be accomplished. Together with the team, this shared passion ignites creativity and hard work necessary to gain the results sought after in an increasingly more global and competitive economy. It is what drives every successful enterprise – a genuine belief in the effort.

Great leadership also involves a necessary love of your team members. The best performing teams genuinely care for each other and go the extra mile for each other. They must in order to achieve extraordinary outcomes and stand out in a crowded marketplace. However, passion just for the people who work with the leader means the mission may suffer. The team is together to accomplish meaningful outcomes. When the team becomes more focused on themselves than the mission, outcomes suffer and competitive advantage is sacrificed.

That is why a great leader has a passion for both – the mission and the people who are carrying out the mission. Together, this love of mission and people produces the best outcomes. My brother, Dave Wolken, is a U.S. Army Colonel who commands a medical unit. I am proud of his service and dedication to both his mission and his people. He routinely reminds his unit about a saying the Army emphasizes, "Mission First, People Always!" As a former military officer, I found this true in successful military organizations. Since leaving the service many years ago, I have also seen this true in my interactions with different successful organizations in various sectors of our economy. And, I have found the reverse true, "People First, Mission Always!" While we are at our jobs, putting people first and always focusing on our mission can help us stand out and be successful in the long-term. When you put people first, teammates and customers respond accordingly. In my opinion and experience, combining love of people and mission is the winning formula.

Keep in mind that there will be times when you lose your passion. Notice it immediately and find it again. From time to time, you may find it important to ask yourself these simple questions. Am I still passionate about my mission and my team? What's missing that will enhance both so we can gain sustainable outcomes? It is important as a leader to find your passion so you can inspire others. Without it, you can only live in the present accomplishing what worked in the past. This kind of existence can feel like drudgery. Passion for your mission and your people will fuel your success!

TAKEAWAYS:

1. You must be passionate as an outstanding Present-Future Leader. Passionate for your mission, purpose, and the people you work with.
2. When you lose your passion, you must find it! Change leadership requires passion.

PRACTICE HABIT:

Ask yourself each day if you are passionate about what you do. If not, continue to change how you work each day until you are.

- 14 -

Love And Kindness As Competitive Advantages

MACNY's longtime Finance Director, Carol Waters, was sick with a life-threatening illness requiring her to take a few medical leaves. We were happy to support her with leave time, given such unfortunate circumstances – it was the right way to care for her. She needed to know we would support her through her time of need. While we did hire temporary finance support for part of her role, the rest of the team responded by working hard to cover for her additional responsibilities. During this time, the team showed love and kindness to Carol and each other. Not only did the team do this the first time Carol took leave, but two more times after that. It truly brought our team together. It demonstrated who we were as an organization and as people. Love and kindness were now firmly part of MACNY's competitive advantage.

START WITH KINDNESS

In today's fast-paced and global economy, can kindness be your competitive leadership advantage? I, for one, think it can be. It takes all kinds to make a community. We all know people along various points of the "kindness" spectrum. And in my experience, those individuals who act with kindness, and are known for being kind, succeed as Present-Future Leaders. Now, that doesn't mean they are push-overs, soft on fundamentals, or oblivious to reality. In fact, it's just the opposite. They are kind despite living in the same competitive and difficult situations as their colleagues and friends.

Good leaders are constantly challenged by striving to do more or succeeding despite the odds. That's why we listen to them, learn from them, and follow them. However, the truly great ones do this with a kindness that makes being with them special and worth the effort. Life is hard. Business is competitive. Troubles are on the horizon – constantly. The true test of a leader is how they handle them. When the leader leads with kindness – everyone notices. It does truly matter. Can they laugh and smile even when the chips are down? Can they find the spirit to care for a colleague or friend when they are hurting? Will they show up and lend a hand when it truly matters? These are ways leaders can be kind.

Great leaders do what they do with a generous spirit of service. Great leaders notice everyone and their contributions, and are grateful for them. Great leaders can be firm but gentle with others when they make mistakes and encourage the person to try again.

These are all examples I have seen of leaders demonstrating kindness. I have been with great leaders who are great because they are both kind and effective. And, I am most certain they would not be so great if they were not also so kind and desirable to be with. Who are your hero leaders? Are they kind? Could greater kindness be your competitive advantage as a leader? Having met so many wonderful leaders, I put kindness at the top of the qualities I look for and so do many of the people I meet. It's a good time to increase your competitiveness – by focusing on being just a little kinder. I guarantee it will make you – and those you lead and work with – happier and more successful.

Love Is Critical To A Leader's And An Organization's Success

Why do leaders shy away from "love" in the workplace? Has it gotten too "taboo" to even discuss the importance of "love" in our lives? Maybe the biggest problem is we overuse the word "love" in our culture to mean everything from love of spouse, children, family, friends, our car, our favorite team, and our cat! Wow! That is quite a span of people and things. Maybe we need to use more precise language in our workplace that still communicates how much we care for each and every meaningful relationship we have in our lives.

First, as Present-Future Leaders, we are best when we care deeply about who we work with and what we are working on. We can feel it when a leader is passionately committed to their team and the mission of their organization. We need more passion in the workplace today than ever before. People are moved by emotion well before they are moved by the facts. We are human beings that feel first – then we engage our brains. Through brain science research, we now know this. We have suspected it for some time. People can see when we "love," or better yet care deeply about people and our mission. People follow people – not the position – and do so out of "love," respect, and admiration.

Leaders and their teams are also whole people who "love" their significant others, their children, and their families. We do best when we honor this and applaud this. It serves us well to recognize this and share our own stories of how we care deeply for others and show it in our everyday life. Again, people respect people first before they will ever follow them in the workplace.

As leaders, we need to find the right way to express our passion, commitment, concern, and "love" – even if the term is overused for so many situations in our lives. We need to find a comfortable way to show it and express it so that, as leaders, we are people who others feel compelled to follow. Besides, it also makes life so much more enjoyable to be around those who genuinely care about others and show it each and every day.

TAKEAWAYS:

1. Love and kindness can bring your team together and be a competitive advantage.

2. As a Present-Future Leader, you need to demonstrate what love and kindness look like within your organization.

PRACTICAL HABIT:

How can you demonstrate love and kindness at work? Make a list you can use to remind you how to best lead by example. Select one and do it today!

- 15 -

NEW SKILLS ARE VITAL

As you might imagine, we have a robust demand for skills training from our MACNY members. Each year, well over 1,000 individuals go through our training and coaching sessions. Almost as many people attend our peer learning seminars. Thousands more learn from our digital content. Why is there so much interest? Employers and their staffs know that they must keep learning to remain competitive – at an even faster pace. Over my 16 years here at MACNY, training has never been in more demand. And, I expect the demand for training to double again over the next two years. And this is just the tip of the iceberg in terms of what companies are spending on upgrading skills.

When the world changes quickly, we as individuals must do so as well. This is one of the main reasons why individuals and teams must continuously upgrade and acquire new skills. The competition demands we keep moving – or else we will fall behind. It's the speed of change that has fundamentally transformed everything we know about work. In the past, we could learn our craft and keep incrementally improving it while we spent a lifetime of work in similar positions producing similar products and services. Past-Present Leadership was all about finding and keeping the best talent who knew what they were doing and how to do it. This is not enough today – companies must hire and promote individuals and teams who are passionate about the growth of their skills and their companies' capabilities.

To acquire new skillsets, an individual must first start with a positive attitude toward and commitment to growth. Each day of each year a person needs to determine what will be needed to excel in the future. Scanning the latest developments in the industry and at a person's place of work is necessary. Having a roadmap and daily plan to learn has never been more critical. Present-Future Leaders must be laser-focused on creating cultures and systems to aid individuals along their paths of growth. This must also happen at the team level. New skills are often needed to adopt new technology, use upgraded computer systems, and work on new products or services. Additional team skills will be needed to ensure that project deadlines are met and new teams are effective in working together.

Often, organizations must create and use new information sharing approaches and systems that must be mastered by all. In an ever-changing marketplace, the newly needed skills will be ongoing. A growth mindset and approach is needed by everyone in the firm. And, as in most things, it needs to be modeled and discussed by the leaders. The Present-Future Leader must be open about their own journey to acquiring new skills. Without it, the team will not believe it is necessary. This could be fatal for the organization.

If an organization fails to create a growth culture and approach, it will eventually lose the race for relevancy. It will appear in a lack of growth at the organizational level. If its people are not growing and acquiring new skills, the company will not grow either. Customers will be lost.

Profits will lag. Talented team members and leaders will leave to find a more growth-oriented company. Losing talent is the worst outcome for growth-oriented companies because companies need incredibly talented people to thrive. Also, a healthy growth orientation makes a company desirable to work at. Acquiring new talent – and their skills – is essential. For a company to be successful, its strategic direction and daily plans must explicitly focus on how individuals, teams, and their leaders are growing – or they'll lose out in creating the future.

WHAT IS YOUR LEADERSHIP LEARNING APPROACH?

Today's competitive business climate requires that we never stop learning – both as individuals and as organizations. Each day, new competitors and old rivals are using technology and new learning to gain a competitive edge. As leaders, we are called to ensure our teams and organizations are also learning and growing. So, what is your leadership learning approach?

Leaders set the pace for change and success in an organization. In order to do so, the leader must identify how they best learn and then adopt these learnings. Being intentional about discovering how you best learn and then making time to invest in new learning and skills is critical. Just as vital, is for you to talk about how you are learning and asking your team members how they are learning and what they are learning. Successful change is a process that we must commit to and we do so when we openly talk about it and encourage it.

I am both a linguistic learner and an auditory learner. I love to read and it is my primary mode of learning that I can do each day. I also listen to learning materials when I drive or do work at home. As a leader, I know it is my job to be intentional about keeping up-to-date and being aware of what is transpiring in industry. What is your preferred learning approach? Have you made a commitment to never stop learning and to do it routinely, if not daily? It is important to know how you learn and to commit to doing it.

Just as important, it is critical that your team knows you are learning constantly and are open to what they are learning and contributing. Do you share what you are learning with your team? Do you ask them how they learn? Do you ask them what they are learning? Do you offer to help them learn and develop?

Today, Senior Leaders are Chief Learning Officers. In a fast-paced world, we all must learn today and implement our learnings tomorrow. Continuous improvement and big leaps in change are now the norm and not the exception. And, it all starts with being a learning leader. By setting the learning pace, we open the door to our teams and organizations winning the learning battle which sets the stage for long-term sustainable growth.

TAKEAWAYS:

1. New skills acquisition by individuals, leaders, and organizations is critical for success in a fast-changing global economy. The organizations that can change fast will stay ahead of the competition.

2. Present-Future Leaders are Chief Learning Officers in their companies and need to lead the way in new skill development.

PRACTICAL HABIT:

What is your learning approach? Identify how you like to learn and begin a daily or weekly effort to acquire the skills you will need to successfully lead your organization or team into the future.

- 16 -

EVERY JOB IS CHANGING

Every job is changing. Not just some jobs as so many people believe, but rather all jobs. This requires us to think and act differently. It also requires Present-Future Leadership to both model this change and help others adjust to this new reality. How much change is now here? Consider the change in cow milking as quoted in *Thanks for Being Late* by Thomas Friedman:

Something strange is happening at farms in upstate New York. The cows are milking themselves. Desperate for reliable labor and buoyed by soaring prices, dairy operations across the state are charging into a brave new world of udder care: robotic milkers ... Robots allow the cows to set their own hours, lining up for automated milking five or six times a day— turning the predawn and late-afternoon sessions around which dairy farmers long built their lives into a thing of the past. With transponders around their necks, the cows get individualized service. Lasers scan and map their underbellies, and a computer charts each animal's "milking speed," a critical factor in a 24-hour-a-day operation.

The robots also monitor the amount and quality of milk produced, the frequency of visits to the machine, how much each cow has eaten, and even the number of steps each cow has taken per day, which can indicate when she is in heat. In the future, a successful cow milker may need to be an astute data reader and analyst.[13]

It is not just cow milkers that must change. Each job is requiring us to use more knowledge and new skills to be successful. Also, jobs that were once held by one person are being disaggregated with some of the tasks going to a higher skilled position, often with the use of computing, and other tasks being assigned into a lesser skilled job and potentially done completely in the future by robotics.

All of this means that the jobs we have today – every job – will be changing dramatically. This change requires us to think about learning and growth differently. We will need to be more entrepreneurial and constantly searching for new opportunities to create and recreate our work, our products, and our services. We will always need a strong foundation in reading, writing, and math, but today's economy also demands strength in critical thinking, communication, creativity, and collaboration.

It seems like a lot for us to do. It is! Additionally, other skills will be needed like grit, self-motivation, and an unwavering commitment to lifelong discovery and learning. All habits and skills I am convinced a Present-Future Leader must have and can master over time.

Individual And Team Growth Must Come First

Where does growth begin? It does not begin at the company level. Sure, leaders can draft up strategic plans and goals but they will go almost nowhere without understanding, commitment, and action at the individual and team level. Growth must be within the individuals and the workgroups and teams they are on. If not, the change plans will fail – sometimes miserably. With individuals focused on growth, an organization can also grow. The team, both leaders and individuals, must be focused on growing themselves first as they grow the company. Growth includes individual skill acquisition. It will also mean new products or services. But, it is highly unlikely that a company's revenues from products and services will grow without the necessary growth of its key team members. Individual and team development must come first. Interaction skills must be mastered. Collaboration and innovation must be a focus. If team effectiveness and individual growth is occurring, organizational growth will follow.

So how do you measure individual growth? It can be measured by the new capabilities and skills the individuals have acquired. The team can also be measured by outcomes that impact new revenue growth and profits. A company cannot sustain growth without its people growing. Another important measurement of team growth is culture—is the company culture supportive of both individual success and team

75

collaboration? When these two areas are tended to, the organization grows and remains profitable. Therefore, successful Present-Future Leaders must spend time on investing in growth. In fact, it must be a major goal of the organization. Also, the organization will need to invest in tools to aid in this effort such as a learning management approach, learning systems, training, and a performance management effort.

As a leader, it is important that the team is passionate about growth. This must include the leader's own growth and development. All effort must be put into getting everyone on the team vested. If not, it will slow or even stop the efforts. Such an outcome is unacceptable. It is better to lose a team member than to let that person stop the necessary growth of the team – and the organization. Individual, team, and organizational growth are all vital to a successful organization.

TAKEAWAYS:

1. Every job is changing – so we as individuals, teams, and organizations must invest in our growth to be successful.
2. As a Present-Future Leader we must focus on individual and team growth first in order for the company to have sustainable growth.

PRACTICAL HABIT:

Examine your existing job. How might it change in the future? What skills will you need to be successful in the future? Pick one of them and start your growth effort immediately. Continue selecting and learning in these key areas to be successful.

- 17 -

HAVE FUN!

I was the S2, or the Military Intelligence Officer, for the 3-17 Calvary Squadron of the 10th Mountain Division. Our unit was deployed to the National Training Center (NTC) at Ft. Irwin in California. We spent three weeks in the desert simulating combat conditions against enemy forces using the latest technologies the Army had. After each battle simulation we would go to the control room for a briefing on how we had done, what we needed to learn, and what our next battle assignment would be. It was exhilarating. It had meaning. It was downright fun!

Are you having fun at work? If not, you are likely falling behind your competition. For many of us Boomers, this makes no sense. We grew up believing that work was work and time off was fun. I remember my Dad saying to me, "It's not supposed to be fun, it's work!" But times have changed dramatically. If you do not have a culture where you are both achieving remarkable outcomes and having fun, you will lag behind your competition – and may actually be putting your company's survival at risk.

Silicon Valley tech companies are known for creating "fun" work environments. They have game rooms, gyms, and actual toys to play with in the workplace. Casual dress codes are the norm. These companies are working to create a culture where doing amazing things and enjoying your work go hand-in-hand. It is certainly different from what I once believed work was all about. My first full-time job out of college was as an Army Officer with the 10th Mountain Division at Ft. Drum. I am sure there were no game rooms in our offices and we did not have casual dress days – or did we?

Actually, we did. I do remember my time in the Army as meaningful and enjoyable. We wore Battle Dress Uniforms (BDUs) which were actually comfortable and much more casual than the dress blue uniforms that were essentially military versions of the business suit. I owned it but wore it infrequently. Our "playground" – so to speak – was the great outdoors where we went to prepare for combat. It was certainly serious – but the best of my commanders made it exciting, intense, and meaningful. I looked forward to those days when we were involved in a training exercise. It was in the Army that I got to drive a tank, jump out of an airplane, go on long road marches, shoot a weapon at the weapon range, and see the world. All this – and they paid me! Our Army units were ready to pay the ultimate price, if called upon. But, what made my time in the Army memorable was another important mission –

inspiring leaders and great people to work together to accomplish great outcomes. When I left the service, I actually missed the great relationships and sense of purpose that we had in my military units. So much so that when I got to lead an organization I worked hard to bring the sense of mission and "doing what we love" into it. Maybe you would not call this fun, but I do.

Thanks to extensive research, we now know that workplaces that are both meaningful and enjoyable produce better outcomes for companies. Leaders who help create and maintain such cultures will outperform those who do not. And, in a world of hyper-competition, this added performance advantage is usually the difference between being successful and struggling.

So, what is the Present-Future Leader to do? Create a culture that is both meaningful and enjoyable! Do it because it will give you an opportunity to have the best team doing amazing things. Do it because you owe it to yourself to enjoy the one life you have—you deserve to have fun while achieving amazing outcomes. Give yourself and others that gift!

RE-ENERGIZE TO ENJOY YOUR WORK

As leaders, we are expected to always be "on." This is a very difficult task to accomplish. And yet, we know we owe it to our teams – and our organizations – to be at our best. Given the stresses and challenges that accompany any leadership role, we must create a rhythm that allows us to continue to excel. How do we do that?

What I have learned is a leader needs to plan and execute times to re-energize. We need to be as committed to rest and recovery as we are to execution and outcomes. If not, we will burn out – and it will show in our performance and in the performance of others. Leadership is demonstrated and our teams do what they see. If we are stressed, our teams will be stressed, too. If we do not take the time to rest and re-energize, neither will our teams. This sets up our teams for eventual failure.

Rest and recovery are the hallmarks of extraordinary performers at all organizations and at all levels. And, it does not "just happen." It's a part of the routine of great athletes, great coaches, and great leaders. However, it may be the part of leadership learning that gets the least amount of attention. How often have you heard a talk by a great performer on how they rested? Rarely. We have countless ways to hear about how a leader does almost every other task. Rest – not discussed. Why is that?

I am convinced it is because it can be seen as a "weakness" by some. Our culture emphasizes outcomes. Rest and recovery is not often viewed as a necessary lead indicator to sustainable achievement – but it most certainly is. Therefore, we as leaders need to build a recovery regimen that we execute daily, weekly, monthly, and annually. We must also encourage our teams to do the same thing. Such an emphasis will result in happier, healthier, and more sustainable organizations – and better business outcomes.

Do you have a way to re-energize? What are you doing to rest and recover? Do you have rituals to re-energize based on your challenges and opportunities? Do you encourage others to develop a routine that allows them to give their best through thoughtful recovery? Enjoy your rest and recovery. It is what gives your leadership abilities the best opportunity to shine!

TAKEAWAYS:

1. Having fun and re-energizing are two critical skills sets of the Present-Future Leader—the success of you and your organization depends on it.
2. Our teams want to both do meaningful work and enjoy their work. If we don't provide this work environment, our best people will seek employment elsewhere – and quite possibly with our competitor.

PRACTICAL HABIT:

When and where did you have the most meaningful and enjoyable work experience? What made it so? Begin today to incorporate the key elements of that work culture into your organization and your work life. Start with even one of the elements and build from there.

- 18 -

ESSENTIAL PREPARATION OF A PRESENT-FUTURE LEADER

A PRESENT-FUTURE LEADER MUST HAVE A COMPELLING VISION OF THE ORGANIZATION

To truly be a Present-Future Leader you must be able to articulate a compelling vision of where the organization is going and how to get there. Leaders are at their best when they are communicating and demonstrating a compelling vision.

Without a vision, the organization and its employees will lack the critical "why" and "what" that are so important to successful efforts. With a compelling mission that lays out what needs to be accomplished, an organization can be successful in the most challenging of situations. This is why you must have a vision for the organization you work for even if your organization does not have a written or universally understood and agreed upon vision. It allows you to lead into the future in whatever capacity you have at your disposal.

Also, the vision needs to be challenged and updated to remain relevant and compelling. Time and time again I see long-standing organizations thrive when leaders refresh a compelling legacy vision and passionately communicate it to internal leaders, managers, and employees. This is a never-ending effort that is necessary for day-to-day and long-term vitality.

Just look at companies like Stickley, Corning, The Raymond Corporation, and Crucible to name a few. Each of these organizations has needed to refresh and update its vision to be successful throughout decades of opportunity and challenge. This took leadership and grit. We are better as a community because their leaders were able to put forth a compelling vision.

So, what is your vision as a leader? Is it compelling for your team and within your organization? Is your vision getting buy-in from the team and driving results that will sustain your efforts? It is never too late to refresh or create and communicate your vision for success. Even if you are not setting the vision for your organization, it is important for you to have your own personal vision for your role.

TAKEAWAYS:

1. A Present-Future Leader must have a compelling vision of where the organization is going. You must be able to communicate it in a meaningful way to others.

2. Great, lasting organizations refresh their visions so they can stay relevant and thrive in a fast-changing world.

PRACTICAL HABIT:

Write down what you believe your organization's vision is or should be. If your organization has an "official" vision, use it as the basis but do not just take it as is. Write your vision in a way you can use it to drive your actions toward the future. Commit your articulation of it to memory so it can shape your current and future behavior.

- 19 -

CREATE A COMPELLING
FUTURE VISION

Present-Future Leaders must create the future with a compelling vision of what their company or team is becoming. Why? The future is created twice. First, it must be created by a leader as a vision of what the organization needs to look like to be successful. Second, the organization must create its vison of the future based on what is actually doable as it lives into the future. In my experience, it is the first future – a leader's vision – that is most undervalued. Too many companies do not have a genuine, well-communicated, and understood future vision of what the organization is becoming.

Why does a company need a vision of its future? Because without it a company may survive, and even be profitable, but will not thrive and remain relevant in the marketplace. Economic forces and competition will quickly overtake the present company business model and a company that is not creating its future will lose out. I have seen it time and time again. Companies without a future vision and plan begin to fall behind. They lose customers in their current business and their new business offerings and customers are not robust enough to secure the future. They can survive for some time, but then a vicious cycle can set in where they attempt to cut expenses to get profitable. They begin to lose key talent to other companies. The culture can even become toxic leading to unhappy and less productive employees. In today's economy, a company must have a future vision they are executing or they are in jeopardy of losing their talent, losing their customers, and losing the technology race necessary to thrive.

Present-Future Leaders are engaged in the present as they create the exciting future with their teams. A Present-Future Leader develops a clear vision of what they, their team, and their organization are becoming. They can articulate it with passion, conviction, and a certainty that inspires hope and hard work. It is an exciting place to be because they are doing meaningful work, enjoying what they are doing, and remaining profitable. People want to work in this company.

A key skillset for Present-Future Leaders is the ability to talk about the company, their people, and themselves in the present as it relates to the future. It's a story of growth they are telling. Growing is what they are all about. Personal, team, and organizational growth is their focus. And, this is why a future vision is needed. It provides a direction and, when properly planned for, a roadmap to the future. As I tell my team, "if you do not know where you are going, any road will take you there." Having a detailed vision is the roadmap needed by thriving organizations.

Creating and executing a future vision can take many forms. It should be rigorous, on-going, compelling, and exciting. It needs to involve everyone on the team and in the organization. So, how do you create your future vision? There are plenty of books and resources on strategic planning. Having a process that is repeated at least annually is critical. However, if it does not create a different future for the company and just lives on a bookshelf, it is not very useful. Ask the following questions about your plans to see if they provide direction for your future:

- Does the strategic plan create a future organization that will thrive in the marketplace?
- Is it bold enough to capture the attention of your customers and team members?
- Is there an execution plan and are you executing it daily?
- Are you keeping score so that you know if you are both achieving your goals and making your organization more viable, profitable, and sustainable?
- Are your team members excited about it?

Every individual also needs a compelling vision of what they are becoming. Sometimes the hardest task in vision creating is getting everyone excited about it, however it's necessary for everyone to be part of it. The future can be scary, but it is less scary if we are creating it rather than just letting it happen. Those who are resisting must be brought into the conversation. Management must talk with each individual, usually privately, so their concerns and issues can be addressed. When they know the organization will do its best to involve them and it is moving forward, individuals will know they have a choice to make – get involved or move on. This necessary process must be thought about upfront so that the team can and will move forward with creating an exciting vision that they are willing to execute.

So, how far into the future must the vision be? This is a very good question. I believe it needs to be far enough into the future to be different than what exists today. And yet, it must also be possible to achieve in the short-term. A future that is too far away carries very big risks. Whereas a future that already exist today – just not in your company – has the greatest possibility of paying out more immediate rewards.

This brings me to how you find your future vision. You can find it just about anywhere. But, it should exist in some form. This allows you to know it is real and doable. Like I frequently say, "the future already exists – it is just not widely distributed." Be on the lookout for what the next opportunity for your company is so you can head toward it immediately.

Once you find a future, how do you know you got it right? You know when your team begins to make progress in executing it – and it's compelling! A future must be an extension of what you can do in the present – just further ahead. There are plenty of examples of the future in next generation technology, services, and products. You want to get there first – or as close to first as you can. Market share can be quickly gobbled up if you get there too late.

One final critical element is that it is important to make the future compelling. Your vision must be rich in details! A detailed vision with a detailed execution plan helps you implement it quickly and effectively. A vague vision without a plan is a dream. Most dreams remain dreams – or worse, become nightmares.

TAKEAWAYS:

1. Present-Future Leaders create a compelling vision of the future so they, their teams, and their companies can thrive!

2. A compelling vision must have the entire team on-board and be detailed. A detailed vision with a detailed execution plan provides the richness needed for quick and effective implementation.

PRACTICAL HABIT:

Create a compelling future vision for yourself. Outline the first few steps to begin the journey. Select one step and begin the journey by creating a daily habit out of it!

- 20 -

IDENTIFY WHERE YOU ARE

Once you have created a compelling future vision –
and a plan to begin to get there – you must clearly
identify what your current situation is. We live in the
present only. Yes, our minds like to be in the past or
future, but we do not actually live in those places. This
moment is all we have and when it comes to our
businesses it is what we are going to do today. However,
because it is built on habits we do each day as well as
routine processes and systems used to do our business,
we often are not fully cognizant of what is occurring. It
just happens each day.

You can ask yourself and your team the following
questions. Do we know where we are? Do we have a
financial picture of our business? Are we profitable? Is
our business growing? Do we have the talent we need?
Are they becoming more valuable each day and year?
How are our competitors doing compared to us within
our market? As you can see, there are endless questions
we can use to better understand our current situation.
And, because we exist in the present, we can get the

answers. But, we do need to actively pursue them. Too many organizations are living in today but are not fully aware of their status—it's easy to be afraid to find out.

It is important to assess your current situation without judgment. See it as an unbiased assessment of a business – any business. There are usually benchmarks and standard measures in our market segment or organizational type. Use those to start. Step back and see just how well or poorly you are doing. If you lead the organization, involve your team so they can clearly see it as well. Don't be afraid of what you will find – teammates have a sense of this already. All the numbers and assessments will do is confirm or modify it. If answered honestly, the question of "how are we doing?" works pretty well to get a gut feeling of where you're at.

It is important to go beyond looking at the numbers of a business. We can get lost in the numbers and even let the numbers convince us we are okay. Asking people for their assessment is often an even more accurate gauge of the true nature of the situation. Don't be afraid to find it out. You really do need to know.

If your current situation is good and your business is healthy than you have the capacity to invest in your future. It may be when the collective organization would prefer to stay where they're at. However, it is the best time to move quickly to the future. Why? You have the resources and strength to do so. But, if you are not in a healthy situation, a crisis can also be a very motivating situation. "Don't waste a good crisis!" is a phrase I remember from early in my career used by leaders to move a team quickly to creating a brighter future.

At the individual level, a leader can also assess where they are at. It is important to do this so you can know where you are as you begin to create your future. Be honest with yourself so you can create the best plan for your future. Ask those who know you well for their assessment. Give yourself the best chance for success. You owe it to yourself.

TAKEAWAYS:

1. A leader needs an accurate assessment of where the business is now so they can effectively create the future.
2. An individual must do the same thing so they can be the leader the business needs to thrive.

PRACTICAL HABIT:

Write down where your business is right now. Look at your financials and assess your talent. Be honest so you can best create your future. Make this a routine habit in order to keep a pulse on your organization at all times.

- 21 -

IDENTIFY WHAT IS MISSING

Once you have identified the compelling futures of yourself, your company, and your teams, as well as assessing where you are at, you can easily identify what is missing. This is a critical step because it is where you must start when creating your future. The gap between the present and the future is what gives you the "what" of your journey. When you do not identify what is missing, your future remains nothing but a dream. Exciting futures are created when you can take actions to transform your dreams into your compelling future.

As a Present-Future Leader, it is your responsibility to help identify and focus the efforts of the team on what is missing in order to achieve the future. A laser-like focus on execution is necessary to move a team out of the comfortableness of the present and into the excitement of the future. Therefore, it is not enough for you to know it as a leader, your entire team needs to recognize it, acknowledge its importance, and move quickly to close the gap between what currently is and what is needed to succeed in the future.

Much of a Present-Future Leader's time should be spent working on what is missing for the future to be realized. What is currently happening will be what an organization focuses on until leaders identify and prioritize working on what is missing. We are creatures of habit, primarily doing what worked in the past. We need to be pulled into the future with a compelling vision and our plan needs to focus on what we will need to do now so it can happen. What is missing is what we work on.

When we keep the future vision in front of us and know where we are, it becomes clear to all we must change. This change is exhibited in our daily, weekly, monthly, and annual efforts as we work to create our future. There are no overnight successes—countless hours will be spent by dedicated teams to make the future vision a reality.

As leaders and teams work on creating the future by focusing on what is missing, the future will become clearer and will likely be different in significant ways from where you started. That is to be expected. A dream is always perfect – but not yet real. The future, in my experience, is even better because it is real, works, and gives meaning to our efforts. Striving for a better future has many important outcomes to include developing the people within the organization and creating more value for customers. It is in the struggles and strivings that we are able to develop and hone our skills as Present-Future Leaders.

TAKEAWAYS:

1. Present-Future Leaders must focus on what is missing between what they are doing now and what their compelling future requires. Otherwise they'll just be managing obsolescence.
2. It is in the struggle of creating the future that we develop leaders, teams, and individuals of excellence.

PRACTICAL HABIT:

Identify what is missing between where you, your team, and your organization are now and what is needed to achieve your compelling future. Pick one item in each of these areas and begin to work on it today.

- 22 -

BEGIN IMMEDIATELY TO IMPLEMENT THE FUTURE!

Start today! Start right this moment! Implement the future right now! Don't wait another minute! I cannot emphasize enough that you can no longer wait to begin implementing the future. Waiting will be the worst possible mistake you can make. Yes, make sure what you are doing is not insane, or hugely risky, or life-threatening. Be smart about it – but do start! When we put change off until tomorrow it is likely to wait for a long time – like forever. Why? In the business world, someone else is moving forward on it today. Somewhere else in this world of seven billion people – someone is moving forward on it. They are creating the future. They are creating – or recreating – their company. Right now!

You may even doubt what I am saying. You may be questioning me, "Really, I can't wait any longer?" Yes, you really cannot. It used to take a very long time for someone to steal your customers – and employees. But, that all changed with the internet. Today, you can reach nearly everyone in the world – as they sit on their couch or in their office. They can research and know more about you – and your competitors - than you know about yourself. This means that your customers are finding their future provider – and employees – right this minute, 24/7.

So, don't hesitate. You must start immediately. But, where does your company start? How do you start? I am sure you have a million questions that you feel must be answered first. However, you do not need to worry. You can start today – and you can just start on you – and no one even needs to know about it.

Why? Because change is instantaneous. Sustaining change is the hard part. Once you know how to sustain the change you want in your life, you can maintain it for a lifetime. You cannot lose by starting in the right way and right away.

The world is changing fast – super fast. Knowing how to change is the skill we all need now. Once we have mastered it – there is nothing we cannot do. The change that is needed is personal change first, which then leads to team change, organizational change, community change, and global change. It really is a chain reaction in that order! When I became kinder to my wonderful wife of 30 years it changed my entire world. When I started planning and executing my top priorities each day, my business changed. When I did these things as a part of my community efforts, my community changed. As my community changes, so does the world.

Pick a hero who changed the world. Please do it right now. Who is it? Is it Martin Luther King Jr., Ghandi, Mother Theresa, Abraham Lincoln, Jesus? Who is your hero? What does your hero have in common with the other people listed above besides changing the world? They did so by acting differently. Yes, they also used words – but they first acted differently and then used their words to help others understand. Change happens because people are different. We say technology changes the world - only if the right people are involved and acting to use it differently. People are the change agents that make the world, our companies, and our families better. Sometimes, they make our lives much better. You can too! But, only if you start right away – even in the smallest of ways.

TAKEAWAYS:

1. As a Present-Future Leader you must begin implementing the future right now. Do not delay. The competition will not wait until you are ready.

2. Start with the smallest of changes needed. No action is too small. You need to learn the capacity to change rapidly to be successful.

PRACTICAL HABIT:

Pick any new, preferably small, and immediately changeable habit. Do it. Now plan to do it each day. Building a habit you can sustain for a lifetime is a skill you must have to be successful. Today is the day you pick and execute that habit.

- 23 -

ESSENTIAL PRACTICES OF A PRESENT-FUTURE LEADER

As a Present-Future Leader, you will need to create essential practices and do them routinely. The practices will vary from leader to leader, but they will be needed nonetheless. In this section I will outline what some of them could and should be. In the following sections, I will outline why your essential practices must become habits, how you turn your essential practices into habits, the value of personal and organizational accountability, and how to keep score of how you and your organization are doing.

You have the ability to change – and so does your organization. You and your organization must in order to survive and thrive. For you to do so, you will need to practice Present-Future Leadership. A Present-Future Leader has an entirely different orientation from a Past-Present Leader. This new orientation requires new and updated concrete practices. So what are some of them?

One essential practice set involves daily reflection, change planning, and future-driven priority execution.

For example, I embed the practices of reflection and change planning into my daily morning, mid-day, and evening routines. My day has become based on executing efforts to create the future.

Most successful leaders I know have daily routines that give them an ability to plan for changes in themselves and their organization. They also execute change efforts on a daily basis to create the future. And just as important, they have a reflection period to assess how they and their organization are doing.

A good part of your time as a Present-Future Leader will be spent creating the future you want today. You will need to identify what you will need to know, learn, and do. That will then spur you to create essential practices. One for me is reading continuously. I read every day. It is an essential practice that I have created as a daily habit so that I can be knowledgeable in my role as the President & CEO of MACNY. I am both changing what I know – and modeling it for staff – on a daily basis. This is a good example of an essential practice you may need as a Present-Future Leader.

You will likely also need some whole-person essential practices to be resilient in times of continued stress and change. Do you have routine essential practices that are focused on physical fitness, meditation or prayer, sleep, and relationships with those you love? If not, you will need to be intentional about building these types of essential practices as well.

One set of essential practices I needed to put into my life was healthy living. I was overweight, inactive, and not practicing good sleep habits. All of this changed over the last two years. I lost and have kept off 20 pounds, I exercise daily, and I monitor and maintain good sleep habits. I am not perfect at any of this, but I am markedly healthier and more productive as a leader because of these changes in my life.

To be a Present-Future Leader, you will need to create new habits, monitor your results, reflect on what you still need, and make adjustments. This cycle will never end. Over the last two years I have implemented over 50 new daily habits and about a dozen weekly habits. And I am not even close to being done. Each week I select and begin a new habit. At work, I have instilled dozens of new habits for our team. And that is also just the beginning. Ability to change is our new skill at MACNY. As its leader, I must model this behavior in all aspects of my life.

Your whole life can change as a Present-Future Leader. You can be a better spouse, parent, sibling, friend, and community leader. Why? Because you are committed to changing what is necessary to become better in all of your life.

TAKEAWAYS:

1. You must change by adopting new habits or adapting your current practices. You will need some essential practices to be successful as a Present-Future Leader.

2. You will need to continuously develop new essential practices. Your journey to the future is on-going and will never end.

Practical Habit:

Write down what you think your new or modified individual essential practices might look like. They should include both work and whole-life practices. You must start changing today. Develop a plan to do so and get started immediately.

- 24 -

THE POWER OF HABIT BUILDING

Each year millions of Americans make a resolution for the new year. Only nine percent are kept. In fact, eighty percent of New Year's Resolutions are abandoned by February – just one month into the new year.[14] Many people have stopped making such resolutions because of the dismal results they have personally achieved — which makes the mere nine percent success rate even more remarkable.[15] So, why do people make such resolutions? People want to change their lives for the better.

Everybody I know wants to make changes that better their lives and the lives of those they love. Yes, everyone! I have never heard someone say that their life is absolutely perfect and they want to change nothing. When people are honest with themselves they can identify what change they want in their lives. They just don't know how to get it.

If change is the desired outcome, then we do know what does work. People who create habits instead of resolutions are successful at change. How do we know this? Because neurobiologists, cognitive psychologists, and other researchers have studied our behavior and have determined that up to ninety-five percent of what we do each day is a habit.[16] We just do it – often times without thinking. Think back on today. Did you make a cup of coffee the same way you did yesterday – and the day before? Did you take the same route to work that you always do? Did you eat breakfast, brush your teeth, and stop by the water cooler like you have done over and over again? You get my point. These are all habits that we just do. Therefore, if you want change to happen and occur over and over again – make it a habit. Let me say that again, any change can happen if you create it as a habit. Yes, any change you want!

The key to establishing new habits again and again is to learn how you best create them for yourself. Any simple habit is a good starter habit. One that works well for me is picking my top three must-do tasks for each day – and a Most Important Task (MIT) from them. It takes me less than a minute to select them after reviewing my upcoming day. It takes me less than a minute to review them each evening. It makes the rest of my day more meaningful and productive. Not a bad return on a two-minute investment of time.

Of course, there is an endless list of habits you can implement in your life that would make you healthier, wiser, more productive, and happier. In fact, any activity you do can most likely be segmented into a series of mini-habits you do each day, week, or month. Complex behaviors like project management and execution at work and getting fit in your personal life are just a series of mini-habits. Again, up to ninety-five percent of what you do is a habit – isn't that where we ought to start focusing our energy if we desire true change?

The other good news is that once you work on a habit it gets easier to do and you can do it much faster. For instance, in January 2016 I started a weekly writing habit of 500 words for distribution to MACNY members. Starting in November 2017, I expanded the habit to 500 words a day. Then, I increased my word count to 1,000 words a day. What used to take me an hour for 500 words now takes me 30 to 40 minutes for 1,000 words. This new habit has allowed me to write this book. Before discovering how I could use habits to change my daily actions, a dream of writing a book would have just stayed a dream. Now, it is a reality that you are reading!

I encourage you to commit to learning how to adopt new habits into your life. Start with one easy habit – and work your way into complex, multi-stage habits. They all work pretty much the same. However, once you know how to do it – you can change nearly everything you choose to do in your day.

If you could adopt just one new habit, what would it be? What would be an easy habit to get the ball rolling for you? What leadership habit could you adopt to help make you a more effective leader? Will you give yourself the gift of change?

TAKEAWAYS:

1. If you want to change your life, do not set goals – create habits. If you create a habit, you can have any change in your life you want – and keep it forever.
2. Start right now to change your life. Learn how to create habits for yourself and you will be able to bring this skill to all levels of your life – and to the people you care about most.

PRACTICAL HABIT:

Make a list of the changes you want in your life. Pick one change you want that is the simplest to do and that you can do daily. Start it today. Keep score that you are doing it each day. Tell someone you care for that you are doing it – and ask them to encourage you to do it each day. This process – repeated – is how you proceed with the rest of your list. You are now well on your way to changing your life on your terms!

- 25 -

THE HABIT CHANGE MODEL

Do you want a way to make sure you implement your must-have habits as a Present-Future Leader? I utilize a simple, but meaningful approach to do just this. To begin the habit creation effort, you must pick what habits you are going to implement into your life. This may seem obvious, but it is where most individuals fail. They do not decide what it is they want to become. They fail to seek the habits that will make them wildly successful. To begin the process, you must decide. Without it, you have decided to not change and will fall behind your peers and rob yourself of the opportunity to be a Present-Future Leader.

Once you have decided what to implement, you must begin – immediately. Start today. A habit desired without implementation is just a dream.

The next critical step is to keep score. Record it once you have done it. In later chapters I will discuss why accountability and scorecards are absolutely necessary to adopting new habits. In fact, I can almost guarantee you will not adopt a new habit unless you keep score that you are doing it. Today there are so many apps and tools available to allow you to keep score of every new change you have in your life. And, you can keep score of nearly everything you want to change in your life.

The next step is to evaluate and make adjustments. When you first start a new habit, you will be less than perfect at it. Guaranteed! But, give yourself credit for doing it imperfectly. Why? You are doing it. Keep in mind that some habits are cut and dry. For instance, I take a vitamin each day. I either did it or not. Others are more nuanced. Practicing calmness is just such an example. Being calm throughout my day is a complex habit. When I review my day, I consider any attempts at remaining calm as practicing calmness. I make adjustments to my approach and start anew the very next day. Not every day is perfect, but I always know that I get to try again tomorrow.

The entire cycle looks like this – decide on habits, do the habits, record when you have done the habits, evaluate your efforts to do the habits, and repeat the cycle again. It is a simple, effective way to begin to change everything you want to change.

This cycle works for any habit. Once you begin to use this cycle you can put habits into your life that you once only dreamed of. Once you get good at putting new habits into your life, you can adopt complex habits that are a combination of mini-habits bundled together such as morning, mid-day, and evening routines.

One of the things I needed to learn was that daily habits are easiest and the fastest to implement. A daily habit very quickly becomes a must-do each day. Why is this? Our brains are wired to repeat habits at a regular interval. We literally create new brain connections with our neurons when we create new habits. And the more we do them, the stronger the connections become, and we become more likely to continue to do them. As you might imagine, less frequent habits take longer to build because the neuron-connections are being formed less frequently.[17] Therefore, expect weekly, monthly, and annual habits to take longer to establish. Anything essential should be created as a daily habit whenever possible.

Of course, you will fail at times. Do not fret over this. Just recommit to starting new tomorrow. Each day you do it you strengthen your neuron-connections making it much more likely you will continue it into the future. Each day you do it is a success. Most habits that don't stick are abandoned too early before they are fully established. Some say it takes 30 days to establish a habit. For some, yes it does. Others it takes much shorter and for some longer. But, what does it matter? If you want to be doing it for the rest of your life – or foreseeable future – then it is just a matter of getting the activity to be at the frequency you need it.

New habits will literally change your life. Once you have this skill, you can change nearly all of your habits. It is one of the most liberating actions you will ever experience. You can replace bad habits with good ones. You can adopt habits you see in your heroes and mentors. You can become the great parent, spouse, sibling, friend, and leader you always wanted to be. So, please do so. Make yourself happier than you have ever thought possible! And, start today!

TAKEAWAYS:

1. Habits are created with a simple process – select a habit, implement the habit, keep score when you did the habit, evaluate how you did, and repeat it tomorrow.

2. Daily habits are easier to implement in your life due to the way our brains work. Whenever possible, implement the habit daily.

PRACTICAL HABIT:

Select a new daily habit, do it today, record you have done it, evaluate how you did, and repeat tomorrow. Any habit that you want – the simpler the better at first – will teach you how to create the habits you want and need to be successful.

- 26 -

ACCOUNTABILITY MUST BE YOUR FOUNDATION!

Without accountability we all fail to accomplish our goals. Accountability is a must! In today's world we must create value and change quickly to succeed. We are highly unlikely to do either without a strong commitment to holding ourselves and others accountable for meaningful outcomes.

How important is accountability? It is critical. Every system needs accountability to keep it focused. Accountability involves timelines, responsible parties, required outcomes, essential activities, analysis of effort, and celebration of success. Some see accountability as a burden – I have come to see it as opportunity. It is an opportunity to reach our greatest desires through achievement!

A Present-Future Leader plays a significant role in creating and living an accountable life. It's not easy to be a leader. We are asked to be enablers and hold individuals, teams, and companies accountable. We offer hope – and realistic assessments of where we are at. It is a balancing act. Sometimes leaders want to be liked more than they want to serve. When we serve, we need to tell others what we see – and sometimes what we see is not what others want to hear. That is why accountability needs to be an important part of leadership. If we have an expectation that we all are accountable and we build systems of accountability, then everyone knows what the expectations are and we can all hold ourselves and others accountable. A Present-Future Leader must lead in being accountable.

Also, a Present-Future Leader needs to let others hold him or her accountable. This can be hard for leaders, especially senior leaders. Everyone needs to hold everyone else accountable for purpose-driven, value-creating outcomes. Some form of public accountability within the team and organization is necessary. Transparency of activity and outcomes gives the entire organization the opportunity to see challenges and seek change. Change and new outcomes are critical to thriving in today's global economy.

You will likely fail at accountability at some point. I know I have. It is human nature to let deadlines and outcomes slip. We can always find excuses. We must not let ourselves get away with it! One of my first lessons as a plebe at West Point was to not make excuses. We were taught to say, "No excuse, Sir/Ma'am." It was a very good lesson. Own your mistakes so you can correct them. Do not take it as a character flaw. Seize the opportunity to demonstrate you can learn and move forward quickly. Leaders need to serve their team, mission, and customers – not themselves!

Once you have committed to accountability, then you must decide how to create habits and systems to make sure it becomes a part of the operating efforts of your company. By now, you know I believe in habits as the foundation of daily human effort. If we want it done routinely and with conviction, make it a habit. Habits are our routines. Individual habits are best executed daily - and the next best is weekly. Team habits are best executed weekly – followed by bi-weekly and monthly. In the next chapter, I will talk about scorecards which create incredible momentum for achieving outcomes. I am convinced that without a scorecard little is accomplished. Create scorecards for the outcomes you must have to be successful. Also, focus on the activity needed to get your outcomes.

Be accountable as a leader. Make accountability your watch-word. If you do so, you and your team will accomplish much of what you set out to do. Success is what comes with accountability!

TAKEAWAYS:

1. As Present-Future Leaders, we need to focus on accountability at the individual, team, and organizational level. Without accountability, we will not be successful.

2. When we have accountability systems in place, we will notice when we fail. That is a good

thing. It gives us a chance to learn and start again as we move toward success.

PRACTICAL HABIT:

Make a list of your most important outcomes. Which ones are you holding yourself accountable for? Pick one outcome you are not yet accountable for. Create a daily habit of accountability for it – and use it today!

- 27 -

SCORECARDS ARE VITAL TO YOUR SUCCESS

Have you ever been to a major sporting event that did not have a scoreboard? I haven't. No one would show up without a scoreboard. There is something in us that just wants to know the score. We want to know if we are ahead or behind. We also want to know critical activity information such as the number of fouls that have been committed or the number of timeouts left in a basketball game. In our organizations, we especially want to know how much time we have left to accomplish our tasks – our timeline. Without a scoreboard there would be no NFL, NBA, NHL, and many more sports we pay to see. Keeping score matters for these successful endeavors – and it does to your success as a person, team, and company.

Every enterprise keeps score in some way. We use financials where we keep score of our resources. Manufacturers keep track of production totals, inventory, and all kinds of needed information so they can be successful. When you define your outcomes and keep score you will also be significantly more successful. Without keeping score, you will fail to accomplish your own change effort. With scorecards, you will be wildly successful.

I had no idea how important scorecards were to creating the future until I started to use them to achieve what I wanted in my own life. Since then, I am obsessed with creating good scorecards and utilizing a scoring system for everything I do at home and at work. As far as habits, if you do not keep score you will not be able to change. Why? Scorecards are the way we implement accountability that we all need.

There are lots of scorecard formats. You probably use them all the time. A checklist is a scorecard of things completed. A watch can be a scorecard of time until our next meeting. We are all using scorecards, but we usually don't take them to the next level so we can change our lives and our businesses. What we need to do is identify the outcomes we want and the key activity it takes to get there. In the book, *The 4 Disciplines of Execution*, they call the desired outcomes "lags" and the critical activity "leads."[18] In essence, if we do the leads (activities), we get our lags (outcomes). Let me illustrate. If I want to be healthy (lag), I must exercise regularly (lead). If I want to be prepared for my day (lag), I must review my calendar each morning (lead). Finding the key activities to get to your outcomes is critical. Keeping score of your leads is how you hold yourself accountable to getting it done. This, in turn, gives you your outcome.

Without scoreboards or scorecards, we do not know if we are accomplishing our goals. Therefore, we need them as individuals, teams, and organizations. In my experience, we need more scorekeeping tools – not less. This is especially true of habits for an individual or team. Leaders need them to drive their own change as well. I use an app on my phone called Coach.me for this. I put my daily and weekly habits on it and I check each of them off when I have accomplished it – each day. It is like a daily checklist that I do not need to write out each day. I have found that I can have simple daily habits like "schedule top priorities" or more complex habits like "remain calm." But, my daily reminder and check off (keeping score) ensures that I do it. Organizations and teams can use checklists, spreadsheets, or their CRM systems to create scorecards of performance.

Everyone should use scorecards and be involved in creating and reviewing scorecards.

They become the best vehicle for conversation, improvement, and accomplishing outcomes. They can also be used for creating new habits. Scorecards can be created for nearly all personal and business change efforts. And it is change that will define our continued success in this rapidly evolving economy. I have learned from my experience that the scorecards should be reviewed by teams weekly. Personal scorecards are best kept on a daily basis. Organizational scorecards should be kept weekly and monthly. Anything longer that that tends to allow for missed opportunities in rapid improvement.

An important outcome of scorekeeping is an increase in morale which accelerates change efforts. Just like it does with a sports team in an actual game. People work harder together and seek better outcomes – a win-win for everyone.

The secret to experiencing rapid change is mastering the use of scorecard creation and re-creation as situations change. Those individuals and organizations that do it well will set the stage for success in today's world.

TAKEAWAYS:

1. Scorecards do for you and your team what a scoreboard does for athletic teams – allows for everyone to know what has been accomplished toward desired outcomes.

2. Scorecards are how an individual, team, and organization implement accountability for key activities and outcomes.

PRACTICAL HABIT:

Develop a personal scorecard – and begin to use it. It will allow you to keep track of your progress toward accomplishing your desired outcomes.

- 28 -

HOW DOES IT ALL COME TOGETHER?

Present-Future Leadership needs to be an integrated approach to be successful. It starts with an understanding that we live in a radically different time than the leaders that came before us. The speed of change is often blinding. The introduction of new technologies is accelerating. Every business is being impacted in some way by global competition and global forces. Every person, team, company, community, and country is impacted. To be successful and truly thrive, we all need to have a Present-Future mentality.

If we don't, our organizations or businesses will quickly become irrelevant. Of course, that does not mean we stop learning from the past as we live today and into the future. In so many ways, we can be successful by applying lessons from the past as we proceed into the future. But even that approach is future focused. A focus on the future is necessary for our success. This book has been all about building individuals, teams, and companies, with a present-future orientation. If we do so, we can thrive. If not, I am absolutely convinced, we will languish and – at best – merely get by. We owe it to ourselves and others around us to do better. We all want to thrive. We will need Present-Future Leaders to lead us there. You can be that kind of leader.

PRESENT-FUTURE LEADERSHIP ALWAYS STARTS WITH THE LEADER

All change happens at an individual level first. Someone has to take the lead for good outcomes to occur. I am a firm believer that every person can be a leader – everyone. In fact, we can all choose to lead or not. No person in any organization is without the ability to lead in some meaningful way. A Present-Future Leader starts with a realization that we are all here to serve others. They understand that to serve others means to never stop changing and growing. It means embracing what will be the future – and moving towards it – always. Speed of change is important, but accepting you will always need to change comes first. Then, depending on the circumstances, you sometimes need to move fast and other times more slowly. But, you will need to change. Standing still is not an option.

The first section of this book was all about recognizing that the future is really now. It is here – it's just not widely distributed. For instance, there are self-driving cars. I just do not have one. But, I likely will – in the not too distant future. Another example, I do not order from a human when I go to Panera – I use an app in the store or on my phone. This is the future of most of the fast-food industry. Not everywhere yet – but likely in many places very soon. In MACNY member companies, robots are working alongside people – today. This will be the norm everywhere very soon. I could go on and on. The future is unavoidable, so each of us must lead from this understanding to be successful.

Also, each leader must use their leadership wisdom – their lessons learned – to guide them in their actions. This allows them to lead in the now. Present-Future Leaders are truly present in the moment. You cannot implement the future any other way. You must act today. You have to use what you see coming and make it a part of your present day. The best leaders I know have their eyes on what is coming – so they can implement today what they will need to be successful tomorrow. And, they do so with passion! They also do it with a genuine care for others. To them, concern and care and love – yes love – are not just words, but actions. They are all-in on what it takes to lead others successfully to the future. They will learn whatever new skills they will need to be successful in the future. They will also help each of their teammates do the same.

And, of course, have fun! Teams that have fun together while they accomplish amazing outcomes are the ones that we all remember. Make interactions with others positive. Smile more. Laugh more. It is what we want in our leaders – authentic people who love what they do, love the mission, work hard at it, and enjoy who they are with and what they are doing. That's the leader

I'd go to the ends of the Earth with. That's the leader I am striving to be. You should too.

To be a Present-Future Leader you must have a vision of where you, your team, and your company are going. What is the future? Remember, the future is created twice! Without the vision of where you are going – the future – you cannot lead. At best, you'll be managing the current situation. It is not leadership to stay where you are and do what you've always done.

Once you know where you are going – you must step back and be realistic about where you currently are. Every person, team, and organization must understand the present. Ask yourself: *How am I doing? What is my current skill level? Where is my team? How is the organization performing?* A deep and honest assessment of where you currently are is critical. Once you know this – then you can prepare to move quickly into the future.

The gap between the present and the future is what is missing. This is what Present-Future Leaders actually work on the most. It must be the urgent task of every Present-Future Leader to correct what is missing to get to the future. Doing what you're doing today is not enough. It will not bring the future. Doing what you're doing today is necessary – but you must be aggressively implementing the future.

Finally, it starts immediately! Yes, right now. You cannot delay in implementing your future. To do so is to fall behind your competitors. Moving is necessary to get to the future – and the sooner you start the better your outcomes will be. Be smart about it and vary your pace when necessary – but move forward. It's where too many companies fail – they don't move forward fast enough on the future they know they must create. This is where Present-Future Leaders are needed. They have a sense of urgency in creating the future!

But, preparation is not enough. You need essential practices to implement the future. The most powerful future vision, knowing what you need to do, and being committed to moving forward will not get you there. Many strategic plans have these elements – and they are still on shelves gathering dust and not being implemented. You need to use the power of habits to create everyday implementation of the future. Present-Future Leaders work on creating habits that make implementing the future a daily, weekly, and monthly occurrence. They also use accountability through the creation and use of scorecards. And these scorecards become a part of their everyday life. Present-Future Leaders plan, prepare, schedule, do, keep score, evaluate, and then repeat this process over and over again.

TAKEAWAYS:

1. Present-Future Leadership starts with individuals who understand the need to go to the future and use their wisdom to create plans to get there.

2. Present-Future Leaders understand and use the power of habits to change themselves, their teams, and their companies. They create a

virtuous cycle of increasing levels of success by planning, preparing, scheduling, doing, keeping score, evaluating - and repeating this process over and over again.

PRACTICAL HABIT:

Begin your plan to create the future as a Present-Future Leader. Create your future first. You can lead from anywhere in an organization. Anywhere! Start with yourself, then your team, and finally the organization.

- 29 -

INDIVIDUAL SUCCESS

If you do not plan and prepare for your success, it will not happen. You must be intentional about your outcomes. Your team and organization must be focused and absolutely committed to changing to stay relevant and to thrive. Without success planning and preparation, you and your company will just drift – and will likely fall behind. Remember, the future is created twice – once as a plan and the second time as it is executed.

One of the things that organizations do too little of is plan for success. Sure, in an organization we say we have a plan for the future – but do we really know where we are going and what we are accomplishing? As an individual, do you have a plan for who you are becoming? What actions will you need to take? How will you know you are getting there? These are all important questions in making your success not just possible – but likely. I am not a big believer in luck. From what I see, people who are prepared and focused get to thrive and then it gets labeled as luck. Sure, circumstances matter – but the luckiest people I know put themselves, their teams, and their companies in a position to thrive by planning and preparing. And, of course, scheduling, executing, and then evaluating their results. This sets up the process to be repeated all over again.

A continuous process of plan, prepare, schedule, do, keep score, evaluate – and repeat is how most thriving people, teams, and companies build success. Although it is not complicated, it is still hard to do. I recommend you start on yourself first. As Present-Future Leaders, we need to model the behavior we expect from others. We must plan and prepare our days, schedule our priorities, do our priorities, keep score, review our daily progress, and commit to doing it the next day. Then, we do the same thing every day from now on – until we change and commit to new habits and outcomes.

To be successful, you must build a success system. Without it, your desired outcomes will be just like most New Years' Resolutions – forgotten and unachieved. Teams and organizations make the same mistake. They do not have a simple, well-articulated process of planning, executing, keeping score, evaluating, and repeating the process – each day, week, month, and year. I have heard it said, "If you do not have a plan, you have a plan to fail." I believe that it is much more likely that even if you have a good plan, you must have a good success system to actually thrive. You, your team, and your business must be clear on how you are going to know you are succeeding.

I can attest to the success of having such a system for myself. I have implemented dozens of new habits in my life and some of them I have done daily for over two years straight without missing a day. How do I know? I keep score. I started with simple tasks like "Be Grateful" and "Daily Prayer" – both habits I could do in minutes. I built a complex but powerful Morning Routine. I added a Mid-day and Evening Routine. I even put more complex habits on my scorecard like "Be Kind" and "Be Calm." Each new habit I placed in my life gave me more confidence and success. I learned how to create, improve, and add new habits. Learning how to change through habit creation has fundamentally changed my success as a leader. I am a different – and better – leader because of it. Once you know how to put powerful new habits in your life, you can have any change you desire.

Over two years ago, I read a book called *Change Anything*[19.] It is worth the time to read. In it are examples of meaningful and dramatic examples of why and how you can literally change anything you want in your life. The chapter that captivated me most was on how to lose weight. Did you know that nearly 98 percent of all weight loss approaches fail? A billion dollar business has been created on the fact that most people will fail to lose and keep the weight off – so they will try again – and again. I was one of those people. Now, if you know anything about me, I do not like to fail. I am wired to find a way to succeed. But, here I was 20 pounds overweight and starting to have health issues. It was time to be successful. I created a set of new habits to both lose the weight and keep it off. I used scorecards to turn my new habits into daily practices. I did not subscribe to a specific diet, rather I built a simple exercise habit into my daily life and cut my calories. And what did I learn? I learned that I could change anything about my life I wanted. So, as soon as I started to lose weight – I went all in on changing the other parts of my life I had always wanted to change. Like writing a book – that of which you are reading.

It has now been over two years since I began my journey to learn how to change my habits. But, each step along the way I knew I would get there. Why? Because I had a system – plan, prepare, schedule, do, keep score, evaluate, and repeat. Looking back – I was not just losing weight – I was learning how to change my habits. Change your habits – change your life!

This methodology can also be applied to teams and organizations. In fact, most organizational change efforts fail because habits do not change. We must do different things if we want different outcomes. Habit change is the only realistic approach to guaranteed implementation. When it's a habit – we do it. Isn't this what we really want for us, our teams, and our businesses?

TAKEAWAYS:

1. To be successful, you must have a system to implement your changes. Use a plan, prepare, schedule, do, keep score, evaluate – and repeat approach. It works like magic!

2. If you want to achieve remarkable change, you, your team, and your organization must be committed to systematic habit change – or you will fail. I have seen it time and time again.

PRACTICAL HABIT:

Begin today to implement your own plan, prepare, schedule, do, keep score, evaluate – and repeat approach. Do it even though you will not be perfect at it. Over time, you will get really good at it. Why? You will have mastered how you go about changing habits!

- 30 -

TEAM SUCCESS

It's at the team level where an organization can really see the impact of Present-Future Leadership. Organizations must move to the future quickly. However, if its individuals are past-present focused they will only do what worked in the past and not be rapidly creating the organization needed to thrive in the future. This is where Present-Future Leadership comes in.

A Present-Future Leader is a model for how we must act on a day-to-day basis. Because they are prepared to lead, they have a vision for what they are becoming and what the organization is becoming. This vision drives their understanding of what is currently being done and what is missing to get to the future. They will use the plan, prepare, schedule, do, keep score, evaluate – and repeat model of action each day. They will be having fun, growing, and doing meaningful work each day. Their very approach – and success – will inspire others to want to act this way also. All real leadership is modeled first. Present-Future Leaders will do this and be the example of what is needed and what is successful in the organization.

Present-Future Leaders will also use the execution approach of plan, prepare, schedule, do, keep score, evaluate – and repeat – at the team level. The team will have a scorecard that gets reviewed each week at the weekly team meeting. It's the scorecard that lets everyone know if the team is being successful! Also, each team member should be expected to have an individual scorecard that they use to measure their own successes. These scorecards need to be created by the team and each individual so they meet the needs of the team and individuals in gaining the meaningful outcomes a thriving culture and organization require. Everybody will begin winning – and so will the organization.

When individuals and teams focus on using transparency around key activities and outcomes, and have honest conversations on problem solving and future building, everyone grows and trust becomes strong. Amazing results are achieved. When this gets multiplied at the organizational level by each of the teams and divisions using the Present-Future Leadership model, the company becomes wildly successful. The company then becomes an attractor of talent and great talent stays only adding to the acceleration of outcomes and success. It becomes a truly virtuous cycle.

Success is inevitable if you use the Present-Future Leadership approach. However, at first, there will likely be challenges until all of the team members buy-in and are enthusiastic about the new approach. It does take time for people to transition to being a Present-Future Leader. Team leaders must be firm but patient with team members as the culture and systems change. Coaching and mentoring will be needed as team members move at different speeds of change. Sometimes, though rare, you will need to remove a team member who will not use the new present-future approach and system. Team members who are committed to learning and thriving in the new approach need to be brought along. Team members who refuse to grow and change and become Present-Future Leaders will need to be removed. It can be painful, but it's necessary for the organization's outcomes to be achieved and for team members to enjoy the benefits of the present-future business.

How will you know team success has been achieved? The team will be contributing to the success of the organization in getting the meaningful outcomes it must have to thrive now and into the future. And, just as important, team members will grow as individuals and enjoy the work environment while working well together. Customers, employees, and the company will all be winning! Who doesn't want that?

TAKEAWAYS:

1. Present-Future Leadership shows just how valuable it is to the organization at the team level. Teams use the plan, prepare, schedule, do, keep score, evaluate – and repeat method to thrive as they create their future organization!

2. When the team is using the system and growing both its team members and its meaningful outcomes – everyone is winning! Team members must learn this new way of working. Although it may take time to learn, it must be used – or team members will need to be separated for the benefit of everyone – customers, employees, and the company.

PRACTICAL HABIT:

Begin today modeling the Present-Future Leader system in your day-to-day work. Use the plan, prepare, schedule, do, keep score, evaluate – and repeat method. If you are the team leader, you will need to implement it in the daily and weekly life of the team. Schedule your weekly check-in team meeting now. Use and build the system with your team each week.

- 31 -

WHAT DOES A PRESENT-FUTURE ORGANIZATION LOOK LIKE?

Present-Future Organization succeeds as it moves into its future. The entire company is focused on creating a company that can live in the present as it builds its future. It does not just accept that it will do today what it did yesterday and make the same products for eternity. The individuals and leaders in the organization are actively planning and executing on what it is becoming. This is often an incremental shift at first, which then becomes more dramatic and pronounced. It's amazing to witness.

There is no one model for how this occurs – but you know it is happening when the company launches new products or breaks into new markets. It sustains a culture that does not just accept what is happening today. Everyone knows it is moving forward to become the future version of itself. But, this transition in the organization does not happen by itself, it takes leaders who are focused on creating just such a business.

Present-Future Leaders need to have a company vision so that individuals and teams can execute it. This vision should be compelling and specific. Leaders who can point to the specific actions needed by the team and its individuals provide for the best chance of success. These kinds of organizations excel in today's economy.

Of course, there will be setbacks. Leaders must push forward. The vision will continue to change – that is ok. It must to stay current with the changing environment. This is why having a future vision is so important. It keeps the team focused when adversity strikes.

I believe it is never too late to begin implementing a present-future effort. However, it will require risk-taking and courage. And, in those moments when courage is displayed, others will see how it is done and follow. The key is to begin within your company today. Each day that is wasted not moving toward the future is a day that is lost to the competition.

Senior leadership is needed to move the whole organization into the future. But, individuals and teams can begin the effort and show the way. Sometimes it is individuals within the organization that begin the effort and others see what is occurring and follow these successes. Move to the future as fast as the organization allows. The movement itself will convince those who are resisting that it will happen. They are more likely to get on board when this is happening.

Companies must move to a present-future focus to stay competitive. As a leader, it is your job to take the bold steps necessary to make it happen!

Takeaways:

1. Present-Future Companies do not accept that what they did yesterday will be enough. They build a future vision that they are actively creating each day. They can see the success of their outcomes and it encourages them to do more.

2. There will be setbacks, but it is important to press forward so the company can thrive.

Practical Habit:

Outline what a successful future looks like for your company. Start where you can today. Use the plan, prepare, schedule, do, keep score, evaluate – and repeat process.

- 32 -

A PRESENT-FUTURE WORLD

If present-future organizations are what we need to thrive, what do our communities, our nation, and the world need? Do we need and can we create a present-future world? Yes! In many ways, we are already creating one!

It is the world around us that contains the future. It already exists, as I said earlier, it is just not yet widely distributed. There are currently communities, parts of nations, and places in the world that are experiencing many of the impacts of future-focused living. In each case, individuals, groups, and leaders are charting a course and have begun to create it. Our task is to look for it, understand it, and engage with it ourselves. For the sake of our children and our children's children, we must become active in this effort.

How do we know where to begin? I like to begin by working with other people and organizations that are actively using the elements of present-future creation. Such people have identified a better future and created a vision to accomplish it, commit to doing it, actually do it, track their efforts, evaluate their progress – and repeat. These organizations are led by Present-Future Leaders and staffed by those who seek a better future. You can tell by their outcomes – they are actively creating the future.

When we lend a hand to these efforts, we learn how to create a better future. We are actually doing it. These cycles are reinforced by our successes and learning from our setbacks. It is rewarding and enjoyable to be doing meaningful work and creating valuable outcomes. At the community, national, and global level, we seek sustainable and meaningful outcomes. Unlike a business, it is usually not about generating a profit. But, rather about fulfilling genuine needs. It involves the necessary resources to grow our efforts and to achieve more success. It is just as important – and usually even more collaborative.

I was blessed early in my career to be offered the opportunity to be the Executive Director of The Samaritan Center in Syracuse. It was a soup kitchen that fed hungry and homeless individuals a hot meal each day. Every day of the week around 150 individuals of all ages would come to our community-financed and volunteer-fueled kitchen and cafeteria. With a small team of five paid staff and hundreds of community volunteers, we did this every day of the year. It was humbling to be a part of such an effort. I would remind our volunteers that it was their warm welcome and smiles that our guest would most need each day. We created community and we satisfied hunger. It was a small piece of creating community – one that cared for its most vulnerable.

But, as its leader, I also needed to help create the future. Through collaboration with other organizations and funders, we began a food services training program to help some of our guests get jobs in the food service industry. The effort supported them with case workers so they could keep their jobs and no longer need our daily meal. We were creating a better future. My favorite part of each day was witnessing the actual serving of the meal. The smiles were so genuine and the concern so evident. Community can be a part of creating the future. In fact, it must if we are to have a better and more sustainable world.

TAKEAWAYS:

1. Present-Future Leaders are needed at the community, national, and world levels to create the future. You can be one by serving with an effort that is already using elements of the present-future model.

2. Creating the future is up to us. We are the ones who must do it – or it will not get done!

PRACTICAL HABIT:

Identify one community effort that has elements of a present-future model. Volunteer to work there. If you already volunteer in such a place, great – do more if you can. Assisting in a present-future community effort changes the community, your nation, and the world – and it gives our lives meaning. It is truly a win-win!

To learn more about the Samaritan Center, visit:
www.samcenter.org

- 33 -

BE DIFFERENT – TODAY!

Today is the very day you can begin being different – happier, more productive, and more successful. It does not have to wait until you are older, wiser, have more money, or have more time. None of these conditions are necessary to begin your new life. It only takes a commitment to begin today. Everyone has the capacity to change – it's just that many do not know they have this incredible power within. It's like having a superpower - but you don't know it yet!

What is this superpower? It's the ability to create habits that you do each day. Who do you want to be? Who do you want to see in the mirror each morning? You can be that person! And, everyone has the capacity. It starts with using your innate ability to retrain your brain. Let me give you a personal example - this very book. I love books. However, I have always thought it impossible for me to write one. The average business book is 40,000 to 60,000 words. That's a lot – especially if you do not know where to start! Then, I started writing a 500-word blog each week. I have done it weekly for two years. Finally, I decided to write a book. I found a coach to help me create a path. I started writing the book daily with between 500 and 1,000 words a day. Two months later my first draft was done! How? I used my innate "superpower" – of which we all have – to create a habit. My brain now tells me to write each day. To be honest, it was easier to write each day than once a week. Why? Daily habits are much stronger. Brain science tells us that daily habits, once established, are like steel cables – they hold us in place doing what we did yesterday.

So, tap into your superpower ability to create a daily habit – any one will do. My personal favorite is Gratefulness. Each day I spend one minute picturing those I love the most and silently calling out their names in a litany of gratitude. I would give my life for these special people. They love me and I love them. Do you think it is possible for me not to smile when I am done? Nope. I do every day. My whole being feels better no matter how early I got up or how tired I am. How long does it take? One minute! How long have I been doing this? 759 days straight as of today! Why? I made the decision to make it a daily habit - and just began. I also kept score of it. That was day one of changing my life. On day two I started the habit of setting my daily top priorities. And yes, I have done that one for 758 days straight – and still going. During the first week, I set many other habits – most small and simple so I could learn "how to change." Once I learned how to change – I could literally change any behavior I wanted. How?

Using the plan, prepare, schedule, do, keep score, evaluate, and repeat method. You can start today! Start this very moment.

Now that you know what your superpower is – the ability to establish a new habit at will – you can change your marriage, your relationship with your kids, your job, and so much more. A Present-Future Leader must always start with changing their behavior. You can become the person you want to be and create the job or thriving company you want to create. And, deep down inside you know you must.

Why not start today? Why not be different? Why not become the leader and person you always wanted to be? You can – I know you can.

ENDNOTES

[1] Ip, Greg. "The Economy Needs Amazons, but It Mostly Has GEs." *The Wall Street Journal*. Dow Jones & Company, 21 June 2017. Web. 14 Mar. 2018.

[2] The Changing Wealth of Nations 2018." *World Bank*. Web. 14 Mar. 2018

[3] Ward, Marguerite. "AI and Robots Could Threaten Your Career within 5 Years." *CNBC*. CNBC, 05 Oct. 2017. Web. 14 Mar. 2018

[4] James Manyika, Michael Chui, Mehdi Miremadi, Jacques Bughin, Katy George, Paul Willmott, and Martin Dewhurst. "Harnessing Automation for a Future That Works."*McKinsey & Company*. Web. 14 Mar. 2018.

[5] Written by Klaus Schwab, Founder and Executive Chairman, World Economic Forum Geneva. "The Fourth Industrial Revolution: What It Means and How to Respond." *World Economic Forum*. Web. 14 Mar. 2018.

[6] "Industry 4.0: The Future of Productivity and Growth in Manufacturing Industries."*Https://www.bcg.com*. 09 Apr. 2015. Web. 14 Mar. 2018.

[7] "Time to Accelerate in the Race Toward Industry 4.0." *Https://www.bcg.com*. 19 May 2016. Web. 14 Mar. 2018.

[8] "Six Sigma and GE: A Story of Successful Implementation." *Brighthub Project Management*. 21 Mar. 2011. Web. 19 Mar. 2018.

[9] Imboden, Durant. "BMW Factory Tour." *Europe for Visitors - Europeforvisitors.com*. Web. 19 Mar. 2018.

[10] Heimlich, Russell. "Baby Boomers Retire." *Pew Research Center*. 29 Dec. 2010. Web. 03 May 2018.

[11] Bosché, Gabrielle. *5 Millennial Myths: The Handbook for Managing and Motivating Millennials*. United States: BeReadyMEDIA, LLC., 2016. Print.

[12] Sinek, Simon. *Start with Why: How Great Leaders Inspire Everyone to Take Action*. London: Portfolio/Penguin, 2013. Print.

[13] McKinley, Jesse. "With Farm Robotics, the Cows Decide When It's Milking Time." *The New York Times*. The New York Times, 22 Apr. 2014. Web. 28 Apr. 2018.

[14] Luciani, Joseph. "Why 80 Percent of New Year's Resolutions Fail." *U.S. News & World Report*. U.S. News & World Report. Web. 28 Apr. 2018.

[15] Seth. "New Years Resolution Statistics." *Statistic Brain*. 15 Jan. 2018. Web. 28 Apr. 2018.

[16] *Using the Power of Habits to Work Smarter*. Web. 28 Apr. 2018.

[17] Pawula, Sandra, Debbie Hampton, Elle, Allanah Hunt, Evelyn Lim, Zeenat Merchant Syal, Lisa Frederiksen, KAMOL Jnr, Debbie, and John Scott. "The

Neuroscience of Changing Your Behavior." *The Best Brain Possible*. 02 Dec. 2017. Web. 28 Apr. 2018.

[18] McChesney, Chris, Sean Covey, and Jim Huling. *The 4 Disciplines of Execution Achieving Your Wildly Important Goals*. New York: Free, 2016. Print.

[19] Patterson, Kerry. *Change Anything: The New Science of Personal Success*. London: Piatkus, 2014. Print.

ABOUT THE AUTHOR

 Randy Wolken is the President and CEO of MACNY—The Manufacturers Association which serves over 300 companies with more than 100,000 employees in a twenty-six county region in Central and Upstate New York. He is also President and CEO of the Manufacturers Alliance of New York, which is a coalition of manufacturing groups representing over 2,500 companies and over 425,000 manufacturing employees throughout New York State.

Randy joined MACNY in 2001 and has dedicated the past 17 years to improving the business climate in New York State. Prior to joining MACNY, Wolken served as the Executive Director of the Samaritan Center; worked as a Senior Budget Analyst in the Division of Management and Budget for Onondaga County Government in Syracuse, New York; and served as an officer on active duty at both Griffis Air Force Base in

Rome, New York and Fort Drum in Watertown, New York.

Randy holds a Bachelor of Science degree from the U.S. Military Academy at West Point and a Masters in Public Administration degree from the Maxwell School of Citizenship and Public Affairs at Syracuse University. He is a graduate of Leadership Greater Syracuse (Class of 2000). He is also the recipient of two Army Commendation Medals, the Lawler Leadership Award from Catholic Charities, and the Syracuse 40 Under 40 Award.

Randy is currently the Co-chair and a member of the Regional Economic Development Council of Central New York (CNY REDC) and the Upstate New York District Export Council. Randy is a former board member of numerous boards to include the NYS Taxpayer Advisory Council, the NYISO Consumer Advisory Council, Onondaga County Industrial Development Agency (OCIDA), the United Way of CNY, F.O.C.U.S. Greater Syracuse, Leadership Greater Syracuse, Brady Faith Center, and the Cornell Cooperative Extension.

Randy and his wife, Dr. Denise Wolken, live in Syracuse and have three daughters.

ABOUT MACNY—THE MANUFACTURERS ASSOCIATION

The 105-year-old organization is the largest manufacturers organization in New York and provides information, human resource services, training, networking councils, energy services, workforce development, public policy support, and political advocacy for its members. About two-thirds of MACNY's members are industrial companies, and the remaining members include accounting firms, insurance agencies, law firms, financial institutions, and other service providers. MACNY aims to assist members in achieving and maintaining their ability to manufacture outstanding products and provide exceptional services, which add value for their customers and lead to sustainable profitability and growth for their business.